*Pleasures of the*

# CANARY ISLANDS

*Wine · Food · Beauty · Mystery*

# ANN & LARRY WALKER

The Wine Appreciation Guild
■
San Francisco

Published by
The Wine Appreciation Guild Ltd.
155 Connecticut Street
San Francisco, California 94107

(415) 864-1202   FAX: (415) 864-0377

*Library of Congress Cataloging-in-publication Data*

Walker, Ann
Walker, Larry
Pleasures of the Canary Islands
Includes Index.
1.  Travel      2.  Wine

L.c. 91-67717

ISBN 0-932664-75-x

Editor: Eve Kushner
Book Design: Ronna Nelson

Printed and bound in
Spain by Cayfosa, Barcelona.

# TABLE OF CONTENTS

# KING HENRY IV

*William Shakespeare.*

## PART II

*(Enter Mistress Quickly, the Hostess, and Doll Tearsheet)*

**Hostess:** I'faith, sweetheart, methinks now you are in an excellent good temperality. Your pulsidge beats as extraordinarily as heart would desire, and your color, I warrant you, is as red as any rose, in good truth, la! But, i' faith, you have drunk too much canaries, and that's a marvelous searching wine, and it perfumes the blood ere one can say, 'What's this' How do you now?

**Doll:** Better than I was!

**Hostess:** Why, that's well said. A good heart's worth gold.

# ACKNOWLEDGMENTS

This book would not have been possible without the enormous help extended by the tourist authorities in the islands who were there when we needed them with answers to our many questions. We would particularly like to thank Mili Delgado and Juan Parrilla Medina for guiding us to some of the secret pleasures of the Canaries.

We are also indebted for the help extended by the Cabildos from each of the islands, as well as the different Patronatos de Turismo, who were: Ricard Tavio, the Cabildo de Tenerife; Francisco Ortega, the Cabildo de Lanzarote; Salvador Borges for his help on the island of Gomera; Victoria Hernandez, the Patronato de Turismo de Gran Canaria; Andres Valeron Hernandez, the Patronato de Turismo of Fuerteventura; Tomas Padron, the Patronato de Turismo of Hierro and Ana Casteñeda, Patronato de Turismo of La Palma.

We owe a special debt to Bodegas Torres of Villafranca del Penedes for the cooperation and hands-on help given by winery representatives in the islands, especially José Grau Ferrer.

# A NOTE TO THE READER

The Canary Islands are unfamiliar territory to most Americans.

"Oh, that place where the birds come from," is the usual reaction.

And that's a pity, for the Canaries offer an amazing array of possibilities: they have the beaches and sunshine of Hawaii or Mexico, the sophisticated cuisine and culture of Spain, the hiking and water sports of California. There are big cities with various international pleasures and remote beaches and woodlands which you may share only with a gull or a sheep.

For the travelers who like to peek into kitchens or tramp through vineyards, the Canaries offer unique treasures. Students of Shakespeare or English history will remember that wine from the Canaries was for many centuries the most popular in England. You can still visit cellars in the islands that are like enological time machines; ancient barrels are filled with the distinctive dessert wines, still made like they were in Shakespeare's time.

Some of the best seafood in the world comes from the Canarian kitchen. The unusual local dishes are the legacy of the mysterious aborigine inhabitants of the island.

Our favorite parts of the Canaries are a bit off the usual path—the small villages and the open countryside—where we met some of the friendliest people in the world. Despite the fact that many Northern Europeans have discovered the pleasures of the Canaries, much of the archipelago is largely untouristed, even sometimes difficult to get to, which is exactly its appeal to the thinking traveler.

It's only a few hours from the lovely beaches on the islands of Gran Canaria or Fuertenventura to the remote mountaintop wilderness of Gomera or Hierro. Each island has a distinct personality, its own charm, and its own pleasures, from quiet walks, looking for endemic species of wildflowers or birds, to windsurfing and skin diving.

This book is not intended to be a complete tourist guide, although there are enough hotels, restaurants and so forth listed to give you a good start. For those who are familiar with our book, *A Season in Spain*, the approach is much the same and this little book could be considered, in some respects, a companion volume to *Season*. It is meant to be a personal introduction to these Fortunate Islands (as the Romans called them), an invitation to discover the unexpected pleasures of the Canaries.

The maps included in this book are merely to indicate the general size and layout of the islands. We recommend the Michelin maps for driving; for hiking in the many parks of the Canaries, a local trail guide is a must, either from the closest tourist office (you will find telephone numbers in this book) or from the park headquarters.

It is perhaps unusual to include recipes in a tourist guide, but since the Canaries are such completely uncharted territory for many, it seemed a good idea to give a more detailed glimpse at the Canarian kitchen. The recipes were gathered from Canarian cooks and have been doubly tested. In some cases, they will have undergone changes in the journey over the Atlantic, since no two kitchens are alike. Translating recipes from one culture to another is always a tricky business, but we have tried to keep these as authentic as possible while meeting the needs of the modern cook. Some ingredients, especially fish specific to the Canaries, would be impossible to find in the U.S. In those cases, we have suggested substitutes similar to Canarian fish.

We also wanted to include recipes because what people eat and the way they eat give real insight into their lives and cultures. We believe these recipes faithfully reflect life in the Canaries.

About bars: there are frequent references here to bars. Put aside all your conceptions of bars as dimly lit places where people go to drink too much and look for romance. The Spanish bar is closer in spirit to the American workingman's bar or the English pub (although the food is much better in a Spanish bar). The Spanish bar is a gathering place where news and information of all sorts may be exchanged or sought. When in doubt about directions, ask at a bar. If you are looking for rooms in a small village, ask at a bar. If you want to rent a fishing boat or diving equipment or catch the next bus to wherever, ask at a bar. In short, it is perfectly feasible to use a nearby bar as a kind of tourist information office. The barman isn't likely to have glossy brochures to hand you, but he is likely to have the information you want. And if he doesn't know, he'll often know someone who does. As almost everywhere in Spain, women and children are perfectly welcome in Canarian bars.

There is no single perfect itinerary for visiting the islands. In fact, the best idea is to make several trips, visiting only one or two islands each time. Travel between the islands is best done by air. There is daily ferry service between Tenerife and Gomera and between Lanzarote and Fuerteventura. Otherwise, the service is slow and unreliable. Iberia Airlines offers frequent flights between all the islands.

The book has a chapter on each island, arranged according to the date the Spanish first conquered it, from Lanzarote to Tenerife.

Finally, the authors have used "I" in this book quite interchangeably. We speak with one voice and it seemed awkward to always use the royal we. Generally, when the reference is to food, the "I" is Ann Walker; when the subject is wine, it is usually Larry Walker. Otherwise, "I" could be either one of us.

# PROLOGUE

*by César Manrique*

I have always been attracted by the mystery that surrounds my land, the Canary Islands. It is true that scientists now agree that the islands were formed by undersea volcanic action, but regardless of such scientific claims, I am charmed by the stories of the ancient Greeks who believed that the Canary archipelago is the remains of the vast, submerged continent of Atlantis.

Whatever their origins, land and water are the essential elements of the Canaries. At every turn, one meets with the vast Atlantic Ocean, which at the same time separates and unites the islands as well as the continents of Europe, Africa and the Americas. The land, formed from fire and water, has in my belief modeled the very character and identity of the Canarian people. Although the islands are isolated and remote, they also serve as a stepping stone between the continents, creating an open, friendly people.

The climate of eternal spring has also helped shape the Canarian people. The islands are blessed with beautiful beaches, woodlands and an abundance of sunshine and food. It is a great privilege, I believe, to live in these islands where one can get along without wearing overcoats or suffering from unbearable heat. We are very lucky here that nature is so generous and provides all that is needed for survival.

I returned to these islands, my homeland, in 1968, called by the volcanic magma, that which has textured my land, a land which urged on me new artistic inspirations. I was further inspired by the wisdom and experience of the people, the artisans and the farmers of the islands. I feel that the greatest art lies in establishing a close relationship with nature, so that we human beings do not take advantage of the earth, ruining it with our ambition, but that we live on it in harmony, using only what we need from it. I feel this is the only way that, in the Canaries or anywhere else in the world, we, the sons and daughters of the universe, can best serve the world. I feel that applying the arts to nature, art in the everyday service of human beings, is the supreme contribution that an artist can make to today's world.

In these islands, I have tried for many years to help bring about this attitude through my art. I have combined architecture with the total environment and with painting and sculpture in an effort to open a new way, a new relationship with the environment, and thereby to create a better community.

*César Manrique is an outstanding international artist who has exhibited his paintings and sculpture in the capitals of Europe and North American. He is responsible for several outstanding total environmental works in the islands, combining architecture, painting, interior design and sculpture. He is a tireless campaigner for stronger environmental protection in the Canary Islands.*

# INTRODUCTION

The Canary Islands are located about 700 miles south of Spain and about seventy miles off the coast of Africa, approximately 300 miles north of the Tropic of Cancer at an average latitude of twenty-eight degrees north. The Canaries are one of five groups of Atlantic Ocean islands called, collectively, Macaronesia. The five archipelagos are the Azores, Madeira, Salvages, the Canaries and Cape Verdes. The Canaries span about 300 miles from east to west, and about half that distance from north to south.

The Canaries are an autonomous region of Spain, divided into two administrative provinces: Las Palmas, or the eastern islands nearest Africa, which includes the islands of Gran Canaria, Fuerteventura and Lanzarote, and Santa Cruz de Tenerife, which includes the islands of Tenerife, La Palma, Gomera and Hierro. Tenerife is the largest island of the Canaries, Hierro the smallest of the seven major islands. There are six tiny islets of which only one, Isla Garciosa off Lanzarote, has a permanent population. The total area of the islands is 3086 square miles, with a population of about 1.5 million.

The islands lie in the path of the Atlantic trade winds, which blow roughly from north to south, making them a natural stepping stone from Europe to Central and South America in the days of the sailing ships. The other common wind is the *scirroco,* which blows straight off the Sahara to the islands, carrying sand and dust so dense that the sun is often obscured, but also creating long, white-sand beaches on the island of Fuerteventura. The cool Canary current flows south-southwest between the Canaries and the coast of Africa.

The islands were built up by volcanic activity from the sea floor over millions of years and were probably never connected to Africa, although there is some speculation that Fuerteventura and Lanzarote, the islands nearest Africa, may have been part of that continent in the distant past. There is still volcanic activity on several of the islands, notably on Tenerife, La Palma and Lanzarote. The most recent eruption occurred on La Palma in 1971.

There is great variation in rainfall among the islands. The Northeast Trade Winds capture Atlantic moisture and dump thirty or more inches of rain annually on the mountains of Tenerife, Hierro, Gomera and La Palma, while as little as two to four inches fall on Fuerteventura and Lanzarote. Most of the rain falls between November and March, although it can be damp almost any time of the year in the northern mountains of the western islands. During the winter months, Mt. Teide on Tenerife is snow-capped, with the snow often lasting until May.

Temperatures are mild throughout the year, again with the exceptions of the mountains on the western islands where it can drop down into the high thirties, especially during the winter months. The hottest time of year is July and August, but even then the temperature seldom climbs above eighty-five degrees Fahrenheit. During December, January and February, it is typically in the mid-sixties to low seventies along the coast, with the ocean temperature ranging from the low seventies to the low eighties, depending on the season. In other words, it is always fine for swimming, diving or other water sports.

## A HISTORY OF THE ISLANDS

*T*he Roman scholar and naturalist Pliny the Elder first called the Canaries the Blest or Fortunate Islands. The name has endured because of their year-round mild climate. The official Roman name was Insula Canum, for the wild dogs found on the islands. Over the centuries, the islands became known as the Canaries, and when the yellow finch (it is actually brown—the yellow bird results from generations of specialized breeding) indigenous to the islands became a popular songbird, it took the archipelago's name for its own. The bird was therefore named after a dog!

The Greeks, who knew the islands and described them with fair accuracy, believed at one time that the islands were the mountaintop remnants of drowned Atlantis. But after the end of the Roman empire, the islands disappeared, at least as far as Europeans were concerned. The Canaries simply dropped off the maps for several centuries, only to reappear in 1375 in the Catalan Atlas, a copy of which is on display at the Columbus Museum on Gran Canaria. The Catalan Atlas shows all the islands in their proper configuration, more or less, except La Palma, which is missing. Tenerife is especially prominent, with the snowy peak of Mt. Teide, the highest mountain on the islands—indeed in all of Spain—sketched in.

There were some raids and chance landings on the islands as early as the fourteenth century, about the time the new atlas would have been available, but the real conquest of the Canaries by Europeans began in 1402, when a Norman sailor seized the eastern desert islands of Fuerteventura and Lanzarote for the kingdom of Castile. Not until Tenerife fell in 1946 did the Spanish rule the whole archipelago.

The conquest was difficult, because the stone age aborigines who lived on the islands put up heroic resistance in some areas. And these aborigines, called Guanches by the Spanish, strike a note of mystery, for it is not clear where they came from or when they arrived. Linguistic evidence indicates that they are related to the modern Bebers of North Africa, but such evidence can be inconclusive. The Guanches on each island spoke somewhat different languages, but could understand one another.

But the real mystery of the Guanches is how they got to the Canaries, since they do not seem to have had ships or even small boats for travel among the various islands. There is no physical evidence of boats, nor did the early Spanish conquerors mention any boats. It is noted in several cases that Guanches *swam* out to meet the Spanish ships. The first reference to a Guanche craft, a dugout canoe made from the wood of the dragon tree and fitted with rough sails, comes almost a century after the Spanish conquest began.

However, up until modern times, the Bebers of North Africa fished near the shore on one-person rafts or mats, made of straw or bamboo. Really, they were more like flotation devices than boats. It is entirely feasible to link several of these mats together for longer voyages, and once out in the Atlantic, to let the trade winds propel the raft to the Canaries. That is, in fact, more or less exactly what Thor Heyendhal did when he sailed an Egyptian papryus craft across the Atlantic. His route passed right by the Canaries. Perhaps the Guanches arrived on the islands in a similar way.

Although it isn't clear when the Guanches arrived on the islands, radiocarbon dates point to the first century B.C. as the most likely time for the main immigration. One discovery, in which charcoal and lizard bones were found together dates as far back as the fifth century B.C. But these remains could have resulted from volcanic activity rather than a Guanche picnic. The history of volcanic activity on the islands, combined with the relative lack of archaeological exploration, could mean that earlier sites simply haven't been found.

The Guanches varied in appearance from island to island but were, in general, tall and fair-skinned, according to Spanish reports. As in Latin America, the Spanish met with no resistance as they intermarried with the native peoples. Within a few generations, the Guanches as a separate people had disappeared; warfare and disease took a great toll, but most were simply absorbed by the Spanish through marriage.

The only reports we have of Guanche culture come from the Spanish, who were not inclined to give much credit to a society unless it produced large amounts of gold. The Guanches lived in caves, except on Gran Canaria, where they built stone and wood houses, and on Hierro, where early reports mentioned stone huts with wooden framing. Caves are numerous in the Canaries because of the islands' volcanic origin.

The Guanches practiced a crude Stone Age agriculture, planting barley, wheat and beans, which were the main ingredients of *gofio*, a ground meal still widely eaten on the islands. They hunted wild pigs, wild cats and birds, and they domesticated goats, sheep, pigs and dogs. They made cheese from sheep and goat milk and rendered pig fat into lard. The Guanche refuse heaps reveal that shellfish was a common food. Nearshore fish were also found, but deep-sea varieties were not.

Despite a low-tech approach to life (goat horns were the major agricultural implement), there is evidence that the Guanche social structure was quite elaborate. According to Spanish reports, all land was held in common. The kings or tribal leaders assigned its use. Each island was ruled by a king or conference of local princes who met from time to time to administer justice, set the dates of various festivals and generally to have a good time. Perhaps, expensive houses are not the highest sign of civilization, after all; if two Guanche groups were at war, the fighting was called off if it were going to interfere with a festival.

According to José Luis Concepción, a Canarian writer who has studied Spanish documents from the period of the conquest, "The Guanches were fond of singing and dancing. They had a place where they would gather to dance and sing. Their dancing was dainty and refined the same dance that is now called "The Canary." Their songs were sorrowful and sad, or tender or funereal, which they called dirges. The latter was to become a famous dance in Europe. It is a dance of request and rebuff, in which two rows of dancers face one another in pairs, they draw close and away again with graceful leaps and taps. . . ."

Guanche laws differed greatly from island to island. For example, on Hierro, a person who committed a robbery had his or her eye put out, but on La Palma, a thief was not punished, as thievery was considered an art. On Gran Canaria, murderers were put to death; on Tenerife, there was no death penalty. On all the islands, crimes against women were punished more severely than those against men.

Containers were made of wood, clay and leather and all tools were stone, because there are no metal deposits on the islands. In fighting, the Guanches used wooden spears with fire-hardened tips, wooden staves and sharp stones, which could be used in hand-to-hand combat like knives, or thrown from a distance.

The Guanche death rituals were elaborate. They mummified their dead. First, they washed the bodies in sea water. Then, people considered unclean and ostracized because of their intimate contact with death removed the internal organs. The bodies were then dried in the sun, wrapped in leather or plant material and buried in caves.

Mummies are not the Guanches' only legacy to the Canary Islands. The Guanches also carved some inscriptions on stones, which have not been deciphered. More important, perhaps, is a legacy of pride in their culture. Recently, there has been a revival of what must be called Guanche nationalism among some of the islanders who claim bloodlines to the Guanches.

# EATING AND DRINKING

*H*ere, we will just briefly tempt you with what's generally available on the archipelago as a whole. Then, as we travel to each island, we will focus on the local specialties.

*Food*

First of all, the Canarian diet is very healthy, consisting to a large degree of fish with a lot of fresh vegetables, salads and fruit. It is a simple cuisine, but it benefits from an abundance of first rate raw material.

Let's begin with some of the most glorious seafood anywhere. The waters around the Canaries are aswarm with fish. One of the world's great fishing grounds lies between the eastern islands of Fuerteventura and Lanzarote and the coast of Africa. There are about 400 species of fish in the waters of the Canaries from almost 100 different families. A great many of these are edible, including at least a half-dozen species of rockfish, a wide range of tuna, including the Atlantic bluefin tuna, the yellowfin, the albacore, skipjack, bonito and mackerel tuna. There are herring, bluefish, sardines, mullet and scores of nameless little "surf" fish often served dried or fried whole. Often, you may not be able to find out the name of the fish on your plate. Best thing to do is simply eat it and not worry about exact nomenclature.

Octopus and squid are very popular on all the islands. There are also mussels, clams and, more rarely, small but delicious crabs. There are no fresh-water fish in the islands, except for a few species introduced as ornamentals or as mosquito-eaters in the small irrigation ponds and reservoirs.

The gardens of the Canaries—based as they are on rich, volcanic soils—yield abundant, delicious crops, sometimes as many as two or three harvests a year. There is every variety of bean imaginable, there are tomatoes, "Irish" potatoes, sweet potatoes, yams and a seemingly endless variety of salad greens. Unlike almost anywhere else in Europe, sweet corn is a staple of the Canarian diet, in the form of corn meal, corn on the cob and whole kernel corn in soups and stews. There are peppers—both sweet and hot—any number of squashes, onions, carrots, radishes. Standard Mediterranean garden herbs grow on the islands, and the orchards yield apples, citrus fruit, mangoes, papayas, pineapples, almonds and bananas.

Canarians commonly eat goat, lamb, mutton, duck and chicken. There are very few cows on the islands and even fewer pigs. There is no large, wild game, but there are rabbits, quails and partridges.

All the islands take pride in local honeys. Many amateur beekeepers have dozens of hives. The standard European honeybee mixes successfully on the islands with some African varieties. There is also a kind of syrup, or "honey," as it is called locally, made by tapping palm trees.

Obviously, the Canarian cupboard is far from bare. But it is fascinating to look more closely at the cupboard to see just how many of these foods have been imported. Most of the dishes originated in Mainland Spain. In addition, raw materials and even entire dishes and recipes from the New World have influenced the Canarian kitchen. Some dishes have journeyed from Mainland Spain to South America and have returned to the Canaries with a new look.

The influence of South America, particularly Venezuela, is quite strong in the islands. Many young people go there looking for work. If they are successful, they return several years later, buy homes and establish a business on their home island.

This Venezuelan connection has led to the following riddle:

Can you name the eight islands of the Canaries?

But there are only seven: Lanzarote, Fuerteventura, Gran Canaria, La Palma, Hierro, Gomera and Tenerife.

Ah, you forgot the eighth Canary island—Venezuela.

Each island has a few distinctive dishes, but some can be found on all the islands. Those include *potaje,* or vegetable, meat and potato stews, soups with *gofio,* a toasted grain cereal, and especially many varieties of mojo, a Canarian sauce that accompanies fish, meat, vegetables or potatoes. Canarian mojo is so successful that it has made its way back to Mainland Spain, where it is often served in tapas bars in Andalucia, especially in Sevilla.

The Canaries have their own tapas bars, as well. Squid and octopus are particular favorites. Just as on the Peninsula (what most Canarians call Mainland Spain), most bars offer the famed Iberico hams from Extramadura. But there is also likely to be a roast leg of pork, *Pata de cochino al horno*, which is thinly sliced and served with the unusually good local breads and cheeses.

In the large cities and tourist resorts of Tenerife, Gran Canaria and Lanzarote, the hotels restaurants offer international menus. In such places, one might encounter mashed potatoes, dyed green or perhaps red, placed around the edge of the dinner plate for no apparent reason other than to get in your way as you try to cut the fish. However, there are some remarkably good hotel restaurants, such as the Hotel Mencey in Santa Cruz de Tenerife, where we have had several outstanding meals.

Italian, Indian and Chinese restaurants are also scattered throughout the large cities, catering to tourists and younger Canarians. The Italian restaurants are by far the most popular and—as in most everywhere else in the world—pizza is a great Canarian favorite.

Despite the Spanish culinary influence, island restaurants run a little differently from those on the Peninsula. The ordinary Canarian restaurant doesn't usually offer as wide a selection as on the Mainland. In addition, while dinner on the Peninsula may not get under way until 10 p.m. or even later, dinner on the islands usually starts about 9 p.m. Lunch also tends to be served an hour earlier, at about 1 p.m.

## *Wine*

So as to have a source of local wine with which to celebrate the Mass, the Church first planted wine grapes in the Canaries. Vines were planted on all of the islands for individual use almost as soon as houses were built. However, there was no commercial wine industry to speak of until the middle of the sixteenth century, when the market

*24*

for Canarian sugar collapsed. Sugar was the first major agricultural export of the islands, with most of it going to Northern European customers. But when the larger, more efficient sugar plantations of the West Indies began under-cutting the price of the Canarian sugar, the local growers were left without a market.

Enter the wine trade, based on the Malvasia grape, a Middle Eastern variety that worked itself to western Europe via Greece, Sicily and Italy. In a warm climate, Malvasia produces rich, alcoholic, full-bodied wines, usually with a smack of sweetness on the finish. Northern Europeans have always had a taste for that style of wine, for "a beaker full of the warm south," as the poet Keats put it.

Canarian merchants using the trading contacts developed in the sugar trade, found that the sweet, high-alcohol wines not only traveled very well, but brought higher prices than the more acidic table wines of France, their chief rivals on the London market. Canarian wines proved so successful that their fame spread far beyond the English and northern European markets. Bostonians called the archipelago, "The Isles of Wine."

As the Oxford historian Felipe Fernandez-Armesto puts it:

"The virtues which made Canary wine so sought-after were admirably summarised by Charles II's historiographer-royal James Howell: "The wines which the islands pro-duced," he wrote, "are accounted the richest, the most firm, the best-bodied and lastingest wine, and the most descated from all earthly grossness of any other whatsoever: it hath little or no sulphur at all in it and leaves less dregs behind, though one drink it to excess. Of this wine if of any other, may be verified that merry induction that good wine makes good blood, good blood causeth good humours, good humours cause good thoughts good thoughts bring forth good works good works carry a man to heaven; ergo, good wine carrieth a man to heaven.

"If this be true, surely more English go to heaven this

way than any other; for I think there is more Canary brought into England than to all the world besides....they go down everyone's throat both young and old like milk."

Shakespeare's fat knight, Sir John Falstaff, and his frequent companion Sir Toby Belch, often lingered over a few "cups of canary." Writing in the 1590s and early 1600s, Shakespeare would actually have been a bit of a trend-setter, as that was the time when Canarian wines were just beginning to be exported. On the other hand, Fernandez-Armesto also wrote: "I think ... there is a hundred times more drunk under the name of Canary wine than there is brought in; for Sherries and malagas well might pass for Canaries in most taverns more often than Canary itself." Perhaps the old knight fell victim to an early wine fraud!

During the seventeenth century, the Canarian wine trade proved extremely profitable. Santa Cruz de Tenerife, the chief wine port, teemed with Dutch, English and American traders. Then, in 1665, The Canary Island Company established itself in London. It aimed to corner the market and create a monopoly in Canarian wines. A group of Canarian wine traders resisted this effort. The dispute greatly increased the wine's price and plunged the market into disarray for some time. In an attempt to bolster prices, the Canary council banned the planting of new vines in 1675. By the end of the century, about 10,000 casks of Canary wines arrived in London every year. But the end was near.

Wines from Madeira were already popular in England when England and Portugal signed the Treaty of Metheun in 1703, giving special trade terms to Portugal and, of course, to Madeira wines. After that, the Malvasia wines of the Canaries went into a long decline. There is some indication that the wine itself also declined in quality, perhaps from overcropping or from the use of inferior grapes in the blend with Malvasia.

There was a brief revival in the Canarian wine trade late in the eighteenth century with a wine called Vidueño. This wine had always been made for local use, but hadn't been exported to any great degree. It isn't clear what grapes were used, but from the descriptions of the wine as thin and lacking in distinct flavor or aroma, it might have been the Palomino grape, still widely grown on the Canaries under the name of Listan. As the world market turned to Madeira wines, someone had the bright idea of making an imitation Madeira from this Vidueño, probably by thickening and sweetening it with unfermented Malvasia juice. This fake Madeira sold for less than half the price of the real stuff and was especially liked in the American colonies, where Madeira was the most popular drink.

All the years of the booming wine trade benefited Tenerife the most. In the late eighteenth century, Tenerife produced four times as much wine as the rest of the islands combined. One can see the faded glories of Tenerife's wine trade in towns like Orotava or parts of Santa Cruz.

Canarian wines had one final spurt of prosperity when Europe was blockaded during the Napoleonic wars. But a combination of cheap wines from Mainland Spain and Italy and the devastation of fungus diseases and phylloxera effectively put an end to the Canarian wine trade before the twentieth century began.

Now, not a single gallon of Canarian wine is exported. Over 500,000 gallons are made for home consumption, although that figure is far from accurate, since much of the wine is never declared for taxation. The real figure would probably be double that. All the islands except Fuerteventura produce some commercial wine, with the best table wines coming from Lanzarote and Hierro. Many of these wines are quite palatable, but high production costs keep them from competing on the world market. Because there is very little money for investment in modern winemaking equipment or vineyards, wine quality is far from uniform. It is discouraging for Canarian winemakers that the everyday wines of Mainland Spain can be sold more cheaply than their wines and generally are of higher quality.

Having said that, though, one should make an effort to

taste Canarian wines. Few ever reach the bottle; most are sold to local restaurants or consumers straight from the barrel. Occasionally, you will find a gem, but one small glass will generally suffice.

It is a pity that someone with the money, expertise and desire doesn't try to recreate the ancient Canarian dessert wines based on the Malvasia grape. It might just be possible to create a niche in the international market for such wines as an alternative to Madeira. When winemakers pay special attention—to both the vines and the winemaking process—the quality of these wines can be remarkable. Several times we tasted superb dessert wines from small cellars, made by winemakers who sold only locally; the wines were like a blend of the finest Madeira and an aged Oloroso sherry, with a marvelous, tangy, nutty quality.

As for other drink, a local beer made on Tenerife called Dorado is fairly good. It is served bottled and on draught. There is a rather harsh rum made on La Palma, and every island has a fair selection of local liqueurs. After a meal, many country restaurants offer a house-made *aguardiente* flavored with various herbs or fruit.

## WHAT TO DO

*W*hat to do on the islands is pretty much up to you. In general, there's just about every kind of water sport you could ask for, from skindiving to surfing. There's hiking, both for the day and overnight, bicycling, hang-gliding, birdwatching and botanizing. And, of course, there's just lying about on the beach or beside the pool. Those who can't go on without daily golf or tennis had better stick to the main islands—Tenerife and Gran Canaria. They are about the only places with large enough flat areas for either sport.

Unlike everywhere else in Spain, you won't find any bullfights in the Canaries. It just never caught on there, perhaps because it was too expensive to import bulls from the Mainland, and because the islands did not have enough pastureland to raise them. On rare occasions, a special bullfighting exhibition is held on Gran Canaria.

Canarians, like other Spanish, are mad about basketball, and teams from the islands and the Mainland play very well. But one spectator sport is unique to the islands—*La Lucha Canaria*, or the Canarian struggle. It's a rather demented form of wrestling, which the Canarians take very seriously, so try not to laugh if you are watching it on local television in a bar. In Lucha, there are eleven very large men on a team. Each person is dressed in what looks like a pre-spandex gym costume—baggy shorts and T-shirts. The object of the match is for one of these large fellows to hurl the other to the turf. In order to do this, they meet in the middle of the fighting area. After shaking hands, they bend at the waist, facing each other, then move cheek to cheek, each gripping the other's shorts. After thirty to ninety seconds of grunting and panting, during which time we expected the shorts to be pulled off, one of the giants manages to topple the other. They arise, shake hands once more, return to the sidelines and allow the next member of the team to come to center court. This goes on for some time. We never did figure out the scoring system, but it was an entertaining half-hour in front of the TV.

There is the usual run of cinema, concerts and drama, but it is unlikely that many visitors make the journey to the Canary Islands to catch the Las Palmas symphony, excellent though it may be.

One of the "sports" we enjoy most in the Canaries is market watching—a visit to the local food market to look at the shoppers and at the fruit, vegetables, spices and other goods on display. The markets in Santa Cruz de Tenerife and Las Palmas de Gran Canaria are particularly good for this pastime. You'll find live caged birds for sale next to freshly-dressed chickens and quail, pots of local honey stacked beside fully-functioning, but closed, beehives. Markets are fun just before mid-morning; the serious shoppers have come and gone, so you won't get in anyone's way when you amble down the aisles like the tourist you are. But there are still enough goods left to give an idea of the full selection. Also, there's always a place to get a cup of espresso and a piece of fruit or local pastry. Markets are a must if you have rented a self-service apartment and are doing your own cooking, which we would encourage. You get the best buys at the market (you can bargain) and the freshest produce.

## WHERE TO STAY, WHEN TO GO

*G*ood hotels are abundant on all of the islands, except Gomera and Hierro. There are certainly places to stay on those two islands, but only a few hotels of international standards, if that's important to you. There are also hostels, pensiones, private rooms and campgrounds. The tourist office on each island can give you lists of private apartments to rent for longer stays, which we believe is an excellent way to visit the Canaries. Living on your own, doing at least some of your own cooking, helps you get into the real rhythm of the islands.

Speaking in very general terms, if you are looking for sunshine, the southern coast of the islands is the best bet. The western islands are substantially wetter, but rain rarely lasts for an entire day. The northern part gets more cloud cover. This isn't as true on Lanzarote and Fuerteventura, which are more influenced by Africa's climate.

There isn't a "bad time" to visit the Canaries. If you are coming to see wildflowers or other botanical attractions, spring is the best time to visit. Otherwise, the temperature swing is not great, at least at sea level, so you can enjoy any activity, whether on land or in the sea, year-round.

# INTRODUCTION

# LANZAROTE

anzarote is the most northeastern of the Canary Islands. At 313 square miles, it is medium-sized compared with the seven major islands—it is larger than La Palma, Hierro and Gomera, smaller than Fuerteventura, Gran Canaria and Tenerife. It lies on the same parallel as Florida and is at some points less than sixty miles from the coast of Africa.

It is also, by all odds, the most unusual of the islands—at least geographically. It is an island dominated by a tortured volcanic landscape, so twisted and broken by the elemental forces of nature that human life—life of any sort—seems almost irrelevant. Yet, in the midst of the jagged badlands of the national park of Timanfaya—suddenly a rabbit pops up—and you realize that life has a way of winning out.

Lanzarote's name comes from a Genoese sailor, Lancellotto Mallocello, who visited the island early in the fourteenth century, but did not attempt to settle permanently. Like its sister island of Fuerteventura, Lanzarote was frequently raided for slaves all through the fourteenth century. Then, in 1402, Jean de Béthencourt conquered Lanzarote, the first of the Canary Islands to fall.

Béthencourt was accompanied by priests, soldiers and two interpreters who had been captured on the island several years before. The Europeans convinced the islanders that they were peaceful and promised to protect them from the slave raiders . There were a few armed clashes over the next few years, but for the most part, the colonization of Lanzarote was peaceful.

According to early chroniclers, Lanzarote was a green and pleasant place, with the trade winds dropping enough moisture to sustain year-round gardens—although given the fact that Lanzarote's highest peak is under 3000 feet, it could never have collected very much rain. Then, a series of volcanic eruptions that began in 1730 suddenly ripped the island's fertile agricultural plain into a broken, rocky plateau, changing the face of almost one-third of the island.

Legend has it that eleven villages are buried under the badlands of Timanfaya, along with numerous small springs and streams. The eruption in 1730 created a whole new mountain range, called the Montañas del Fuego or mountains of fire. The real wonder of Lanzarote is not the fierce assault of nature, but how the people of the island have survived in the face of such spectacular destruction.

## Beachcombing

Volcanoes are not the only story Lanzarote has to tell; there is an incredibly beautiful coastline with both black- and white-sand beaches (the white sand has blown across from Africa), some very fine local cheeses, seafood and wines.

Almost every mile of Lanzarote's shoreline is a beach lover's delight. When I took a close look at the map and saw mile after mile of great beaches, I wanted to settle in for a long stay, just to get to know them a little better. With Lanzarote's mild climate and relatively f.at terrain, backpacking would be a perfectly feasible way to explore this coastline, which is mostly unaccessible with an ordinary car.

Beginning near the international airport between Puerto del Carmen and Arrecife, one can beach hop around the island, never being more than a few kilometers from the next—probably deserted—playa. Puerto del Carmen, for example has a white-sand beach that appears to go on simply forever. One can amble down the Avenida de las Playas (Avenue of the Beaches—plural on beaches—that should give you an idea of beach availability) with good restaurants on one side and miles of beaches on the other.

If your taste runs to more primitive or at least less built-up beaches, then put on your hiking shoes or rent a four-wheel drive vehicle and check out the wild west coast of Lanzarote. A string of great beaches runs from Punta Ginés through El Golfo, La Isleta, and even past that, right up to the northern tip of the island. There are hiking trails in Timanfaya park and many hikers follow the dirt tracks down to the deserted beaches of the west coast from El Golfo, where there is also open camping as well as the best swimming on the island.

You can charter boats for fishing and diving at several harbors on the island, including a good one at Puerto del Carmen. Fishing is first rate all around the island. Diving is good as well, with a professional school at Puerto del Carmen.

Windsurfing is a major sport on Lanzarote. It is good at Puerto del Carmen, although it is best on the north coast of the island. There is also board surfing in the north at Playa de Famara.

## WHERE TO STAY

*T*here is no dearth of hotels on Lanzarote. Most are concentrated on the island's southern half, clustered around the resort areas of Puerto del Carmen, Costa Teguise and the capital of Arrecife.

Some tourist guidebooks give Arrecife a bad time, one describing it as modern and messy with a "surfeit of potholes." Well, it is all those things, but one can hardly blame it for being modern. And one person's 'mess' is another person's 'charm.' The potholes can't be explained away—perhaps the island's government has other priorities. But the real problem with Arrecife is the contrast it presents to the rest of Lanzarote.

On an island of such great natural beauty and, in the

desertlike parts, almost supernatural tranquility, Arrecife and the surrounding urban area, a stretch of perhaps ten to twelve miles from Puerto del Carmen in the south to Costa Teguise in the north, seem somehow awash in hustle and bustle. However, we once stayed in the Los Zocos in Costa Teguise, a four-star hotel geared in all ways to deal with tourists, and found it exceptionally quiet and peaceful. A long white-sand beach was just across the road. We could watch the sunset from our balcony. And, if we wished, we could have prepared our meals in the room with provisions from a grocery store within the complex. It's true, that approach to travel is not for everyone, but it was relaxing. There are dozens of such hotels and apartment complexes in the area.

But even this area, a so-called tourist sprawl zone, is gradually being subjected to a very tough set of new planning controls. These were inspired to a large degree by the Canaries' most famous artist and conservationist, César Manrique, a native of Lanzarote.

Outside of the developed tourist area, there are many small towns where lodging can be had. One of our favorites is the pretty little town of Haria in the "valley of one thousand palms." Haria is only a few kilometers from Las Bajas (a bay with excellent windsurfing and small-boat sailing) and a series of fine beaches. Haria has no tourist hotels, but there is a hostel on the main square and several houses have "room for rent" signs in the windows. You can look for similar lodging in Tinajo, Famara, Teguise and Yaiza.

## Camping

No camping is allowed inside the Timanfaya national park, but, as elsewhere in the Canaries, there is informal camping; simply locate the landowner or caretaker and ask permission

# EATING AND DRINKING

## The Food

An immense variety of seafood, excellent goat and sheep cheese, good rabbit dishes as well as kid and lamb can be found almost anywhere. But the seafood steals the show. A specialty of Lanzarote is salt-dried fish and various octopus dishes.

## The Wine

The vineyards of Lanzarote are an amazing sight. They are unlike any vineyards we have seen elsewhere. Rainfall has always been low on Lanzarote, so even before the fateful eighteenth century volcanic eruptions, farming must have been touch-and-go. After the lava covered the most fertile part of the island, you would think everyone would simply have thrown up their hands and left it to the goats and rabbits. Even they must have a hard time living in such a lunar landscape!

But the black volcanic cinders or *picons* (they look a great deal like palm-sized lumps of coal) are actually the key to agriculture on Lanzarote, especially in the vineyard. The cinders condense moisture from the night dews, depositing a tiny but steady trickle of water into the soil beneath the gravelly volcanic dust. The amazing vines of Lanzarote are planted in craters, dug into the volcanic debris and surrounded by stone walls two to three feet high, called *zocos*. Each crater is some eight to ten feet in diameter and contains one vine. The tough roots of the vine, nourished by the steady supply of water, penetrate the lava to the buried soil. The stone wall protects the vine from the wind and slows the deposit of sand into the crater, although it must still be dug out every few years to keep it from burying the vine.

Wine grape growers are unanimous in their belief that a vine under stress produces wines of higher quality; if this is so, then the wines of Lanzarote would be the best in the world. However, other factors besides stress lead to fine wine, so a vintage Lanzarote is not a threat to the fine wines of the Penedes or Rioja regions of Spain, or to wines from California or France. But Lanzarote wines are quite pleasant, especially the Malvasias, both dry and sweet. Indeed, there are few finer treats anywhere than a glass of slightly sweet Malvasia taken directly from a cask behind the bar, served with a hunk of goat cheese and maybe a plate of marinated octopus.

## WHAT TO DO

Look for wildflowers in the northern regions, especially on the high plateau known as El Jable in February and March.

• Bicycling is very popular on Lanzarote. It is one of the flattest islands in the Canaries and we saw more bikers there than elsewhere.

• One of the newer sports is hang-gliding.

• You can soak up the rays on hundreds of beach and, if all else fails, go ride a camel in Timanfaya park.

. . . . . . . . . . . . . **SNAPSHOT**

*Having just flown in from Tenerife a few hours before, we decided to enjoy an early dinner and a sound night's sleep at Los Zocos Hotel in Costa Tequise. We went to the hotel's restaurant where the food is decent, the atmosphere quiet. At the next table, four Britishers were obviously in a mellow, holiday mood. Our dinners were moving at about the same pace and when we ordered a Torres Spanish brandy after dinner, they were curious about it and we fell into conversation.*

*It turned out they were all old friends who had bought a*

*time share apartment on Lanzarote eight years before. Every January, they spent two weeks together, enjoying the surf and sun and exploring the island. They traditionally ate their first-night dinner on Lanzarote at the Zocos, just across the street from the apartment.*

*"We really love it here," one of the women said. "We have friends back in London who can't imagine how we can go to the same place year after year. But the fact is, there is so much to do on Lanzarote that we never get all the things done we set out to do before it's time to go."*

*At that point, the hotel manager (whom we knew slightly) stopped by to see that all was well. I told him about the people at the next table and their tradition of a first night dinner at Zocos.*

*He promptly treated us all to another round of brandy.*

*"Lanzarote? I'll tell you about Lanzarote. There's 60,000 goats and damn-all else."*

*—A disgruntled Brit at a bar in Puerto del Carmen.*

*He was right about the goats, otherwise as wrong as he could be, as you shall see.*

Perhaps the first stop on a tour of the island should be the Monumento al Campesino, a huge white abstract sculpture rising starkly out of the fields in the center of the island, about ten kilometers from Arrecife, near the small town of Mozaga. The monument, created by César Manrique, is dedicated to the peasants of the island. There is a restaurant at the monument, The House of the Campesino, which serves authentic island cuisine and local wines at very reasonable prices. It's a good introduction to the island's cuisine and yesterday's lifestyle.

There's also a museum with uncertain opening hours, which features many artifacts of the island's past, including a fascinating working model of what they call a water closet, which is not at all the same as what the English call a water closet. Reclaimed or stagnant water is poured slowly over a porous volcanic stone. The water drips through the stone into a potted plant, then percolates slowly through the potted plant and drips out into a container below, where it is regarded as 'purified.' These water closets are found all over the Canaries, but are especially common on Lanzarote, where water is very scarce.

On both Lanzarote and Fuerteventura, houses are built with nearly flat roofs that become, in effect, water collectors. The roof is scrubbed down, with fresh whitewash applied each year before the brief rainy season. Water falling on the roof is directed by a slight slope of the roof to a drain where it is stored in small, above-ground reservoirs. Water is so rare, that in the days before desalination increased the domestic water supply, neighbors would borrow used potato water to boil their potatoes.

Beyond the Monumento al Campesino, follow the road toward Yaiza, where the main highway turns back toward toward the Parque Nacional de Timanfaya. The road takes you through the area of La Geria, where you can see vines growing out of craters. If you stop the car to inspect these curious vines more closely, be sure the shoulder is firm, not loosely packed volcanic gravel.

These fields are an incredible sight, with widely spaced vines, each defended by a circle of stone. The yield of grapes per acre is quite low, of course, which makes the wine rather pricy, compared to the Peninsula wines. It is a bit awesome to consider the enormous amount of labor involved in making these wines; it is an indication of how important wine is in the culture of Lanzarote and the Canary Islands. And not just any wine, but local wine, wine from the hometown soil, so to speak.

Wherever Mediterranean people have gone, the wine grape has gone with them, no matter how difficult or discouraging the cultivation might be. We saw this every-where in the Canary Islands, surely one of the more difficult places on earth to grow wine grapes and make wine, yet there it was, the grape and the wine.

Wine has been a part of Mediterranean civilization and culture for so long that it is difficult to understand why it so

often comes under attack by prohibitionists and those who equate it with illegal drugs, seeing it as an evil force in the world. Yet, again and again in our visits around the world, we have seen that in areas where wine is the common beverage, there is little or no drunkenness. We have visited the small country villages and large cities of every island in the Canaries, and nowhere did we see anyone drunk, except in set-aside tourist areas where vacationers from the U.K., Germany and Scandanavia were found. And their drink of choice was not wine.

On Lanzarote, a truly heroic effort is made to wrest this beverage of moderation, of civilization, from a harsh soil. The wines are not world class and, after a glass or two, one is glad to return to the outstanding wines from the Spanish Mainland. Yet wherever I am, I find myself lifting a glass of wine in a silent toast to those determined farmers and wine-makers of Lanzarote and I am reminded of the ancient toast:

"Water separates people, wine brings them together."

End of lecture.

Beyond those stony vineyards, the village of Yaiza is a pleasant, whitewashed town; one could easily be in North Africa from the looks of it. There is an unpaved road just beyond Yaiza that leads to the small village of of El Golfo and its spectacular cliffs and beaches. El Golfo's lagoon is an emerald-colored, crescent-shaped body of water formed in a half-collapsed volcanic crater. When we were there, the road to the lagoon was blocked, but it's only a short walk to the beach where weird twisted volcanic rock sculptures have been carved out by the wind. It's a beautiful sight, as the lagoon nearly glows like a jewel below the jagged cliffs. There are several restaurants in the village, all serving excellent fresh fish and local wines, as well as a good selection of wine from the Peninsula. Try the Restaurante El Golfo, in particular.

From Yaiza, take the highway north, toward the Mountains of Fire. You are deep in the volcanic badlands here. There is very little life in this twisted landscape, although several species of lichen and wild Geranium have managed to dig in their roots and hang on. There may be a lizard, the *Lacerta atlantica*, or a few rabbits who probably wandered in from the cultivated land at the edge of the badlands.

Hiking is forbidden in the park, first, because it is dangerous (the rocks are often precariously balanced and a bad fall is entirely possible), and second, because park officials realized that almost everyone who visited Timanfaya was carrying away a piece of the park. They reasoned if that continued, there would soon be little park remaining. Keeping people on the roads at least discourages such mindless souvenir hunting.

You can take a guided bus tour of the park. The buses leave from the visitor's center at Islote de Hilario. Or it is possible to take a short camel ride for a close-up view. Camels actually worked on Lanzarote until after World War II, as they did to a lesser extent on Fuerteventura. The camel's large splayed hoof is perfect for walking on the soft volcanic soils of the island and, of course, the beast was also valued as a desert animal, able to work long hours without water.

Today, camels are a tourist attraction. It's quite a fun ride, if short and somewhat bumpy. Each camel carries two people, one on either side in a basket slung over the camel's hump. It shouldn't be missed!

The bus ride may sound a bit mundane after trotting about on a camel, but, in fact, it can be pretty exciting as well. The bus takes some fairly sharp corners on the narrow road and there are times when one literally hangs over the awesome emptiness of a crater. There are thirty-six craters within a five-mile triangle.

After all that sightseeing, you'll be glad to know there is an excellent restaurant at the park headquarters, again in a Manrique-designed Mirador, called the Restaurante El Diablo (a grinning devil with a pitchfork is the park's symbol). The restaurant is built in the round, so one has a wonderful view of the Fire Mountains and the sea.

The specialty is fish grilled over a volcanic vent directly under the restaurant. It's a bit uncomfortable to realize that you are actually sitting on top of an active volcano while you sip your wine and nibble at the excellent grilled sardines.

The menu consists of, among other things, Potaje Canarias, a thick soup or stew, new potatoes in their skins, mojo sauces, wonderful grilled fish such as fresh sardines or Cherne fillets, soft and succulent or grilled meats. Everything is simple but well-prepared and the service is very relaxed.

The restaurant not only serves tourists, but also accom-
modates Lanzarotenos who often bring their own food to
cook over the volcano-powered grills, then take the finished
dishes to a nearby beach.

Well out of the volcanic badlands and to the north lies
Teguise, the first capital of Lanzarote. Here, the island turns
noticeably greener. The soil is still volcanic, but it's much
older and has more vegetation. With vegetation come
goats—Lanzarote's 60,000 goats. If goats are not properly
pastured, they can be a little rough on the landscape. But
bless them for all that wonderful cheese!

As on the other islands of the Canaries, the first capital
was built inland, as a defense against pirate raids. (Presumably,
pirates were too lazy to walk a few miles.) The old capital
of Teguise is a wonderful spot for a few hours of walking
around. The town takes its name from the daughter of the
last Guanche king of Lanzarote. She married Maciot de
Béthencourt, the nephew of Jean de Béthencourt.

With cobblestone streets and whitewashed buildings,
the small town seems suspended in time. The locals (natives
of Lanzarote call themselves *conejos,* or rabbits) have done
what they can to stop progress here. It takes a special
permit—which is very difficult to obtain—to make any
changes in the buildings.

The town encourages local artisans and craftspeople
with various tax incentives. A municipal market on Sunday,
which offers everything from fresh fruit to paintings and fine
jewelry. One of the most famous products of Teguise is the
*timple,* a small four- or five-stringed guitar. You can also find
red clay pottery at the market, based on Guanche designs.
Another popular item at the market is a modern copy of a
Guanche fertility symbol. It's a flat-headed, seated figure
with both male and female sexual characteristics.

El Meson de Paco, near the central plaza, is one of the
oldest buildings, almost three centuries old. It has been
lovingly restored with an art gallery on the first floor and a
good restaurant upstairs.

There's a good view of the northern part of the island from the Ermita Las Nieves, a whitewashed hermitage overlooking the sea and the northern area known as El Jable. Nearby is Haria, a largely untouristed village where white houses straggle up a valley, contrasting picturesquely with splashes of green from the palm trees.  This valley is known locally as theValle de las Diez Mil Palmeras, or the Valley of Ten Thousand Palms.

Beyond Haria, the road more or less comes to an end at the Mirador del Rio, another Manrique design perched high on a rocky cliff, overlooking the small islands of Graciosa, Montaña Clara and Alegranza.  Of the three, only Graciosa has permanent inhabitants; about 500 people live there, although hundreds often ferry over for a day trip from the village of Orzola on Lanzarote's northern tip.  Graciosa is under very tough planning controls; unless you were born on the island, it is impossible to get a permit to construct a house  or a commercial building on the island.  There is a wonderful sand beach on the island, virtually deserted much of the time.

The channel separating Orzola and Graciosa is about a mile across and is called *El Rio*, or the river.  It was here that the conqueror Béthencourt first anchored.  Orzola itself is a pleasant fishing village with several good seafood restaurants and boats to charter for fishing and diving trips.

From the heights of the Mirador, you can quickly descend to the depths, or even below the depths, into two caverns formed by volcanic action.  The *Cueva de los Verdes* formed thousands of years ago when volcanic gases blew out a mile-long tunnel of lava that had earlier filled a dry river bed.  The caves, which lead to the sea, served as hiding places for the Guanches and later for colonials fleeing raiding pirates.  Including all the side tunnels and branches, the underground system contains more than four miles of galleries, one of the longest known volcanic caves in the world. The guided tour takes about one hour.

Nearby is another cavern, the *Jameos del Agua*.  It formed

when sea water rushed into a hot lava fissure underground and turned to steam, blowing out an "escape valve" in the hillside and opening the cavern to the outside. The landlocked lagoon within the cavern hosts a species of blind crab, found nowhere else on earth.

The story here is not about the spectacular natural beauty of the cavern, but about how it has been transformed into a unique tourist center by—once again—César Manrique. After working for over a decade, from 1965 until 1976, he has developed an underground auditorium and concert center and a restaurant. Several multilevel walkways surround the lagoon and lead from one part of the cavern to the next. With a few thoughtfully-placed lights and plants, Manrique has turned the 650-foot long natural volcanic hall into something like a subterranean cathedral, a truly special place.

Manrique's latest project is as different from *Jameos del Agua* as the sun from the moon. It's the *Jardin de Cactus*, or cactus garden, now being developed a few miles north of Costa Tequise. Manrique has collected varieties of cactus

**WINDMILL AT RIDGE OF CESAR MANRIQUES LATEST CREATION, THE JARDIN DE CACTUS ON HIS NATIVE ISLAND OF LANZAROTE.**

from all over the world to be planted in a garden shaped like an amphitheater, with reflecting pools bridged by footpaths. As the cactus garden matures, it will be used as a study center for those interested in cacti. The government expects that it will attract scientists from all over the world and become, in time, a major horticultural center.

It is typical of Manrique's genius that his creations are shaped and adapted to the environment, whether the environment is water and stone, as in the Jameos del Agua, or sand and sun, as in his cactus garden. Manrique has said that the artist must work to protect the environment against the excesses of technology. He incorporates nature into his work in such a way that his creations seem truly organic, born from the earth itself.

Changed first by volcanic explosions, and again by Manrique's artistry, the landscape of Lanzarote keeps evolving. While the same can be said of much of the ever-developing Western world, Lanzarote looks almost untouched by human influences. The sand from Africa keeps amassing on the beaches, the goats continue to breed and munch on the vegetation, and the rugged badlands stand as a monument to that which people cannot affect. To visit Lanzarote is simply the kind of experience that is available hardly anywhere else in the world.

## USEFUL INFORMATION

Tourist Information, Parque Municipal, Arrecife: 928-81 18 60.

Diving and fishing, Clubunlanza, Puerto del Carmen: 928-82 60 61.

Four-wheel drive expeditions to remote beachs can be arranged through Explora in Costa Teguise: 928-81 36 42. A day trip includes lunch and a guide with every vehicle.

Almost any kind of water sport, from sailing to diving and windsurfing can be arranged through your hotel desk. In the north, ask at La Santa Sport in Tinajo: 928-84 01 01. This is a time-sharing apartment complex but, for a fee, nonresidents can arrange windsurfing lessons and the like or obtain information on where to find them.

# FUERTEVENTURA

uerteventura is the second largest of the Canary Islands, after Tenerife. It is rather sparsely populated, with about 25,000 in all. Of those, probably 5000 are members of the Spanish Sahara Armed Forces or the Spanish Foreign Legion, which were stationed here several years ago during Spain's Saharan problems with Morocco. The capital, Puerto del Rosario, has a population of about 15,000, so that doesn't leave very many Fuerteventurans to occupy the rest of the island's 660 square miles.

The island is a bit over sixty miles long and about twenty miles across at its widest point. It's only about fifty miles from Africa at the nearest point and is the driest of all the Canary Islands, due in part to natural influences and in part to human ones. There are magnificent beaches on the island, miles and miles of white sand virtually untouched on both the east and west coasts. However, the west coast tends to have more rocky beaches than the east, where sand from the Sahara blows ashore, forming the beaches.

Like all the islands, Fuerteventura was well-known to slave-traders in the fourteenth century, but no real effort was made to colonize the island until 1404, when Jean de Béthencourt conquered it for the Kingdom of Castile. Fuerteventura was the second island after Lanzarote to fall, following a series of skirmishes in which the Guanche aborigines retreated into the interior and resisted for a few months before laying down their arms, mostly wooden spears and large stones. The populations of both Lanzarote and Fuerteventura must have been seriously weakened after over 100 years of slave-raiding and looting by Spanish and

Arabic traders. It was the price the two islands paid for having relatively good harbors and being the nearest of all the Canaries to Africa.

The island could be called the island of goats, because huge herds roam freely across the landscape. This may be why there is so little water on Fuerteventura; unchecked goats destroy vegetation, which cuts down on evaporation and thereby reduces precipitation. Indeed, the capital was called Puerto de Cabras, the Port of Goats, until 1957, when the name was changed to Puerto del Rosario, Port of the Rosary, probably as much for aesthetic as for religious reasons.

## WHERE TO STAY

*F*uerteventura is looking to tourism as its main industry for the future, so there is an abundance of places to stay on the island, often relatively inexpensive. Rentals range from modern resort hotels in the south, to beach cabanas almost anywhere, to long term housekeeping units in giant complexes all along the more accessible east coast.

Fuerteventura, like the other islands, encourages tourist areas to be built as separate complexes, outside the existing towns and villages. Borrowing a British term, they call this 'purpose-built' housing. While this segregation of tourists does protect the outlines of native island life to some extent, it creates a potential problem for those who want to break out of the tourist mold and find the real Fuerteventura.

Actually, having a non-touristy stay isn't as difficult as you might expect. Keep in mind that all distances are relative. It's perfectly feasible to have a comfortable bed and shower in one of the tourist resorts and to spend sixteen hours a day exploring the rest of the island. It is also possible, with a little poking and prying, to find very reasonably priced apartments and beach houses for a week or longer within the mainstream of island life. It's the same old story—ask at the bar or ask the taxi driver. Or keep your eye out for signs in windows saying "Rooms to rent."

## *Camping*

Although there are no official campgrounds on Fuerteventura, there is a lot of freelance camping. We saw hundreds of campers on the beach. Fuerteventurans are easygoing people, and unless you abuse the privilege of camping by trashing the beach or some other outrageous behavior, it's a simple matter to stake out a few yards of pristine white sand and set up housekeeping for a few days.

## WHAT TO EAT AND DRINK

### *The Food*

The island has an incredible abundance of seafood with such bewildering nomenclature that it is virtually impossible to always know the name of the fish on your plate. Among those that would be familiar to Americans and Europeans are several varieties of sea bass, or rock cod as it is called on the American west coast, haddock, mackerel, cod, swordfish and an abundance of tuna, including albacore, bluefin, skipjack and yellowfin. Then, too, the rich African current that runs between Fuerteventura and the coast of the Sahara yields a huge number of fish that most of us have never heard of or seen before.

Country bars and restaurants often serve a myriad of small, dried surf fish, or *pejines seco*. Perhaps a half-dozen fish or more come to the plate. They need simply to be peeled and eaten whole. Dried octopus and squid are also tapas. On the fishing beaches (which are the rocky, cobble beaches—the tourists get the sand beaches) the little fish and the octopus are hung out to dry like clothes on a line. The octopus and squid are brought to the customer on a plate in the more upscale bars, but are put directly on the bar (many of the bars have galvanized tin tops) and set ablaze in the blue collar bars. The barman simply pours a few ounces of high-proof neutral alcohol over the octopus, snaps his cigarette lighter and it's instant octopus flambé. He keeps turning the fiery bits with a fork until the flame subsides for an even toast. Wait a moment for it to cool and you have a tasty, crunchy snack.

Goat and kid, sheep and lamb are also regulars on the Fuerteventuran dining table. Sheep and goats travel together in free-roaming herds on Fuerteventura and usually appear on the same menu. Rabbit, either wild or domestic, is available in the country too. But it is in the wide selection of seafood that the island really shines.

There are hundreds of good restaurants on Fuerteventura. All of the major hotels have their own restaurants (at least one) where it is possible, should you so desire, to order from an international menu. In the small villages and the countryside, simply follow your nose.

## The Drink

Fuerteventura is the only island in the archipelago that has no commercial wine production. We saw only a few vines in kitchen gardens. Wine is brought in from neighboring Lanzarote as well as from the Mainland. Even in the smallest country bars and restaurants, you can find good Riojas and fine wine from the Penedes area of Spain.

## WHAT TO DO

*B*egin with the beaches: white-sand beaches, cobble beaches, black-sand beaches—many visitors begin and end there. Off the beaches, there's excellent windsurfing, board surfing, deepsea fishing, sailing and scuba diving. In the remote west, there's hiking, camping and a fair bit of bird watching.

. . . . . . . . . . . . . . **SNAPSHOT**

*We were at our favorite table at the Restaurant Los Caracoles in Pozo Negro. The Atlantic was almost lapping at our toes. A half-grown lamb and a puppy, probably about the same age, were wandering around the tables, sniffing at this and that. The puppy found more to eat than the lamb. Earlier, the lamb had been tied to a post, but the owner had turned the lamb loose to forage, after a table of four well-dressed Spanish from the Mainland had left in their rented Mercedes. We were the last table still outside, lingering over a Torres brandy.*

*A waning moon was rising out of Africa, casting a dim light down the beach, over shadowy fishing boats. The whitecaps of the low breakers were just beginning to catch the moonlight, which was almost the only light in Pozo Negro. A white light flickered over the sign of the village's other restaurant a few hundred yards down the beach. Way up on the hill, a few lights were visible in the dozen or so tourist bungalows.*

*Inside the restaurant, a late dining table of a half dozen or so had also gone on to cigars and brandy. Someone in the party was quietly playing a timbale, a musical instrument common on Fuerteventura and Lanzarote. Shaped like a small guitar, it's played like a mandolin and produces a soft, plaintive sound. I looked with some satisfaction at the ruins of our dinner, including a huge platter of fresh mussels that had been served with a delicious mojo verde. We invited the owner to join us for a brandy and a cigar, which he did.*

*I waved toward the lamb. 'Will it be on the menu one day soon?' I asked.*

*He grinned, pouring another brandy all around from the bottle on the table. (In the country restaurants of the Canaries, as in Mainland Spain, the brandy bottle is often left at the table and you pay according to how much is depleted.)*

*52*

'No, never. That lamb is an orphan. She is my little love. When she is older, I will put her out to pasture with the rest of my flock. I have over forty sheep and about 150 goats back up there.' He waved toward the dark hills behind us, the malpais grande, the big badlands.

' We took it in when it was only a few days old and fed it from a bottle. Its mother was killed up on the highway. The puppy there, he is the same age as the lamb, born in the same week. They get along well. If the puppy bites too hard in play, the lamb turns around and kicks him.'

I started to light a cigar, which I had bought earlier that day in Puerto del Rosario, when he motioned me to stop.

'Wait. Let me get cigars from the bar. I have some very good ones there.'

They were very good cigars indeed, handrolled by a friend of his from the island of La Palma.

'But the leaf, that is not Canarian. The leaf comes from Cuba,' he said.

We smoked in silence for a time, watching the moon climb higher above the sea. Somewhere in the malpais grande a dog was howling.

As he poured a final round of brandy, he said, 'I saw you making notes earlier. You are a writer?'

I told him that my wife and I were planning a book about the Canary Islands.

'You like it here?'

'Very much,' I replied.

'Good. You must tell other people to come. But not too many. And just those who will respect what we have, our quiet, our solitude. Tell them to come, but only if they will respect us.'

Fuerteventura has a double appeal. First, it is a beach lover's paradise, with mile after mile of white-sand beaches, as well as some very inviting black-sand playas. There are over 150 named beaches on the island, but a determined

# FUERTEVENTURA

hiker or someone with a four-wheel drive vehicle (which can be rented at the large hotels) would have no trouble finding hundreds of unnamed beaches—how often do you get the chance to name a beach? Naturally, every kind of beach activity is available.

The island will also appeal to those who love the desert, especially the desert landscape typical of the American southwest. The mountains of Fuerteventura are not high—

the tallest peak is Pico de Zarza in the southern section of Jandia at 2646 feet—but they are rugged, with deeply indented canyons leading down to remote beaches.

There is a constant play of light and shadow on the mountains, with the colors changing according to the angle and intensity of the sunshine, ranging through all the purples and light violets.  There is a stunning fifteen kilometer drive from the lovely old town of Pájara to Betancuria, which was one of the island's first capitals, designed by and named after Fuerteventura's conqueror.  The highway twists through the central mountain range, winding up and down steep dry *barrancos* with traces of old terraces carved out of the rocky hillsides.  Then it drops down into a spectacular mountain valley known as theVega de Rio de Palmas, or the Valley of Palms, where the intense greens of the irrigated, palm-filled canyon contrast richly with the bronzes, purples and deep blues of the surrounding barrancos.

The best way to begin a visit to Fuerteventura is by sea from the island of Lanzarote, Fuerteventura's desert island neighbor to the north.  There is a thrice-daily auto ferry from Playa Blanca on Lanzarote to Corralejo on the northern tip of Fuerteventura.  The 8 a.m. ferry is a very pleasant way to begin the day.  As on the other island ferries, the espresso is excellent and just a tiny nip of anis or brandy in it will fortify you against the forty minute sea voyage.

There are good views of both islands during the trip and the ship passes quite near the Isla de los Lobos, a tiny islet a few miles off the north coast of Fuerteventura that is now a national park.  The island was originally named for the sea lion, which is called the wolf of the sea in Spanish.  These sea-going mammals once bred on the island, but no longer.  Lobos is one of the best areas in the Canaries forswimming and diving and boats can easily be rented in Corralejo for a day trip to the island.  There is a restaurant there called Casa Antonio, run by the lighthouse keeper.  If Antonio takes a liking to you, he may be willing to fix a paella, made with seafood taken from the ocean only minutes before.

However, if Antonio doesn't happen to take a shine to you, there are other possibilities in the tiny hamlet of El Puertito. Perhaps the most enjoyable way to spend a few hours or a day on Lobos is to pack a picnic from Corralejo and to enjoy the tranquility of the fine sand beaches. There is also excellent fishing all around Lobos, especially in the two-mile wide channel between Lobos and Fuerteventura, known locally as El Rio. For transportation to Lobos, ask around the harborside at Corralejo where the ferry from Lanzarote docks. You'll have no problem finding a boat either for a day trip or for a fishing excursion off the island.

Having disembarked from the ferry at Corralejo, take a short walk around the harborside to get your land legs back. Although the once-small fishing village is rapidly growing into a mid-sized tourist town, there is still a core which stubbornly refuses to be overwhelmed by bright lights and discos. It is a startling contrast to see grizzled fishermen, usually sporting a stubble of beard and dangling a cigarette from their lips, mending a fishing net on the dock exactly as generations of fishermen have done, while a few hundred yards away on the white-sand Playa de Corralejo, pale-skinned and naked tourists slowly bronze.

There are several major tourist hotels on the Playa—it seems that about one a month goes up—and it's perfectly possible to explore the island from a base at Corralejo. However, a more central location would be Puerto del Rosario and its immediate area. The airport is only a few kilometers south of the capital and there is a Parador Nacional between the airport and capital. Furthermore, the Playa Blanca at Rosario is just as inviting as the beach at Corralejo, if somewhat smaller.

South of Rosario, there is a major 'purpose-built' resort complex at Caleta de Fustes centered around the eighteenth century water tower of Castillo de Fustes. The tower was designed to fend off pirate attacks, including at least one foray by the Englishman, Sir Francis Drake. One wonders what those pirates would make now of the sprawling complex with its swimming pools and children's play-ground, much frequented by the hated English.

There is a beautiful beach at Fustes and a protected yacht harbor where it is possible to charter boats for fishing or diving for the day. The apartments are pleasant enough. Most have tiny kitchens, which you would do well to ignore, as good restaurants are remarkably cheap and plentiful on the island.

Having centered yourself somewhere near Puerto del Rosario, you can start your explorations. There is very little in the way of public transit on the island, but there are rental car agencies at the airport, all major hotels and near the ferry terminal at Corralejo. Rates at local agencies are much cheaper than at international agencies. Gasoline is expensive (as on all the islands), but it takes a long time to use up a tank of gas on Fuerteventura.

South of the airport along the coastal highway and just past the turnoff to Caleta de Fustes is the small, almost abandoned village of Salines, caught in a time warp; even though it is only a few hundred yards off the highway, the village seems stuck solidly in the nineteenth century. There's nothing in particular to recommend Salines, except a kind of New England austerity, a sense that nothing much has changed in several centuries. There is a nameless bar-restaurant featuring simple grilled fish caught straight from the sea that morning with the ever-present mojo sauce on the side.

Back on the highway, the road quickly turns inland. The countryside here is relatively flat and is a bit like west Texas, with goats and sheep instead of cattle and oil wells. After eight kilometers there is an intersection; turn left, back toward the coast and the fishing village of Pozo Negro. This is one of our favorite places in all the Canary Islands, although it's hard to explain exactly why.

The protected beach—part cobble, part sand—is not extraordinary, but is usually empty. It's a nine kilometer drive from the intersection over a highway that passes through a jagged 'malpais', a volcanic landscape where sheep and goats have the right-of-way. The paved highway ends abruptly, several hundred yards from the beach. An unpaved road to the left leads to the northern edge of the playa and goes over a steep mountain pass back up the coast, rejoining the paved road just south of Caleta de Fustes. That route requires four-wheel drive. The bumpy but easily passable road to the right leads past some old outbuildings to the central part of the beach where there are two small restaurants. Up on the hill to the right are a few modern beach bungalows, rented semi-permanently to Germans and English.

We've seen surfers trying the waves in Pozo Negro, but the real attraction of the place is to wander among the dozens of small fishing boats pulled up on the beach and overturned, fishing nets spread across their bottoms. But watch your head—a half-dried octopus flapping in the breeze on the upper beach could smack you in the face!

One morning, we arrived in town needing a cup of coffee badly before driving south. Neither restaurant was open, but by banging persistently on the door of Bar Los Pescadores, we aroused a young man who had been cleaning the kitchen. He invited us in out of the wind, made us a cup of espresso and sent us on our way in good spirits, refusing to take any pesetas, since, "After all, we are not open. How can I take your money?"

Back on the highway, follow the signs to Tuineje and Gran Tarajal. At Tuineje, you can hang a right toward Pájara, which means 'tiny hen.' This small town has one of the most pleasant central plazas in all of the Canaries, the Plaza Nuestra Senora de Regla. The quiet, tree-lined plaza with a prominent church and town hall is the true center of the town's activity. First built in 1645, the church is quite interesting. It has a huge carved stone doorway, part of the original structure, with an unusual Aztec-inspired geometric design.

Just up the main street from the plaza are several good

bars for tapas. It being late morning, we settled on skipping lunch (since we were planning a major seafood dinner in the fishing village of Caleta del Cotillo that evening), but decided to fill up on substantial tapas.

We got right to business in the Bar Tio Pepe, ordering a chilled bottle of Torres Viña Sol, a tapa of calamares seco, the dried squid set aflame right on the bar before us (watch your wine glass) and a tapa of the pejines seco, the little dried fish which are peeled and eaten in bite-sized snacks like popcorn. These treats are a specialty of Fuerteventura, the barman said, adding that he dried his on a rooftop line. The two small plates were just right as a snack, but we still had some wine left in the bottle. In an effort to get the wine and food to come out evenly, we ordered a ration (about half a normal serving) of grilled Sancocho, an African fish with a firm, white flesh. It was served with a green picante mojo sauce, richly flavored with cilantro.

The drive from Pájara to Betancuria is truly magical. The town of Betancuria is like a fresh oasis of lush gardens and orchards, due to a high water table that has maintained itself so far, despite having several windmills pump day and night.

Although modern Betancuria is some ten or twelve rough mountain miles from the coast, Jean de Béthencourt originally established it on the coast as a defensive bastion against the raiding pirates. Finally, when the attacks became too much of a nuisance, he moved the entire city inland.

The town winds down a gently sloping road above the canyon below, with the church, the Iglesia Santa Maria de Betancuria, standing like a sentinel on the opposite side of the canyon. The church has an interesting wooden Canarian balcony, apparently held to the whitewashed wall by supernatural means, for no other support is visible. In the interior, there are three aisles and a marvelous statue of St. Catherine, which is said to be the oldest church relic in the Canary Islands. There is also a statue of the Virgen de la Peña, the chief attraction at the town's June festival and the patron virgin of Fuerteventura.

There is a remarkably good Museo Arqueologico with several rooms of Guanche and early conquest artifacts. The collection of Guanche pottery is particularly interesting. The rooms surround a central courtyard filled with native plants and the museum itself is in an old house, possibly dating to the seventeenth century. Opening hours are irregular, but the caretaker lives in the house opposite. You could also ask in the bar-restaurant next door, where there is a pleasant outdoor dining area overlooking the green canyon below.

North of Betancuria, the road winds through the Valley of Inés where you can see several whitewashed windmills from the highway. Many more huge iron and tin windmills have come from Chicago, ceaselessly pulling the dwindling supply of underground water to the surface.

About twenty kilometers north of Betancuria, the main road continues back to Puerto del Rosario. Take the paved road to the left toward Tindaya and La Oliva. At the intersection, there is an unpaved road to the left, leading to a memorial tower for the Spanish poet, novelist and philosopher, Miguel de Unamuno, who was exiled to Fuerteventura for a time in the 1920s. He fell in love with the bleak, desert beauty of the island and wrote several poems in its praise, calling it "an oasis in the middle of civilization's desert."

A few kilometers north, follow the signs to Tindaya. There's a nameless country restaurant at the intersection with outdoor tables where you can sample an excellent, sharp, local sheep cheese with wine and bread. In fact, you can watch perhaps the very sheep that produced the milk to make the cheese as they steadily graze away inside a stone-walled enclosure across the street. The sheep are, as usual, mixed with goats with about a nine-to-one ratio of goats to sheep.

· · · · · · · · · · · · · **SNAPSHOT**

*It was late Sunday morning in an attractive bar-restaurant in the quiet town of Antigua. There were only five or six people there. We were all sitting at the bar, most with an espresso, though one old farmer had a tot of rum on the side. We were planning our day, studying a road map and wondering if our rented Ford sedan could make it on the dirt road between Antigua and Betancuria, when a giant tour bus pulled up in front of the restaurant.*

*Within seconds, so it seemed, the entire place was filled with large young men, ordering espressos or beer, shouting back and forth, looking for the toilets, asking to see the menu, in general, being noisy and putting out a great deal of energy.*

*But within ten minutes they were gone, leaving in their wake a few dozen empty coffee cups and beer glasses, a couple of abandoned newspapers and a great sense of quiet.*

*'That was a football {soccer} team from Madrid,' the barman said. 'They are here to play an exhibition match tomorrow, but today they have been taken on a tour of the island. They will come back later for the lunch they ordered.'*

*'Ah, and what are they having for lunch?'*

*'Goat. Every one of them wants goat for lunch. And where am I to find all that goat on a Sunday morning?'*

Back on the main highway toward La Oliva, a small town best known for the eighteenth century former governor's house. The Colonels' House or Casa de los Coroneles has recently been restored after lying in ruins for years. It's a rather grand looking building for such a tiny town.

Beyond La Oliva, follow the road to Cotillo with perhaps a brief stop in the small village of Lajares. The tourist shop there has some examples of local embroidery. But don't linger too long. It's almost dinner time, which should be welcome after a long, dry run from Pájara and the flaming octopus tapa.

From the highway, Cotillo seems an unlikely place, with a few small shops and unappetizing looking bars. But once off the main road, it takes on an entirely different aspect. Follow the unpaved road north of the town and keep going north. The road was in an odd stage of construction when we drove it, with one side paved, the other basically sand. Several beach chalets have been constructed and it is likely that the entire road has been paved, right up to a small lighthouse, Faro de Tostón. Several of the finished houses were for rent and they were considerably more tasteful than most tourist beach developments.

There are dozens of tiny rocky coves and inlets all along the road, with sandy mini-beaches sandwiched between the rocks. Dozens of people had pitched tents and were camping all through the area. The campsites are spectacular at sunset with the sun dropping into the Atlantic.

Back in Cotillo, we sought out Casa Juan, a tiny restaurant filled with an amazing potpourri of German and English students (probably some of the campers), small children and dogs, local fishermen, blue collar types and a car full of well-heeled Mainland tourists who had driven over from Corralejo or Puerto del Rosario.

Casa Juan, about fifty yards from the sea, serves some of the best seafood dishes anywhere. Once inside, secure a table and a bottle of wine. They have a good selection from the Mainland as well as wines from Lanzarote and Hierro. Then go to the kitchen and poke your nose into the various pots sitting on top of the stove. You can choose from soups, stews and sautés. Fresh fish is at the front counter; choose one and say how you want it cooked. If you are a little short on Spanish, pointing is perfectly okay. There is also a self-service section, a cross between a salad bar and a deli.

We started with a great white bean salad with minced green peppers, onions and slivers of ham. Then came grilled mussels topped with a little mojo verde, a parsley and garlic sauce that mingled with the mussel juices. We dabbed at the juices left on the cast-iron platter with chunks of bread. The Sopa de Canarias was chunky, full of potatoes, sausages and garbanzos with lots of rich broth. Grilled fish—so fresh they seemed to still taste of the sea—and tiny new potatoes in their jackets came with the same green sauce. More good dunking with the bread ensued.

From Puerto del Rosario, it's easy to explore the miles and miles of beaches on the southern tip of the island. These white-sand playas, the main tourist bits around Morro del Jable, stretch for almost fifty kilometers from Punta del Colorado to Faro de Jandia, the lighthouse at the extreme southern tip of the island.

Head south on the main coastal highway, only this time follow the sign to Antigua, reluctantly turning away from the coast and Pozo Negro. In only a few kilometers, take the smaller paved road to the left toward Valle de Ortega, a pretty little upland town where it's probably a good idea to stop for tapas. There is a typical local sausage there with a touch of fresh herbs that is excellent when grilled with fresh tomatoes on the side.

Back on the road, pass once more through Tuineje, then follow the signs toward Gran Tarajal, the island's main southern port. Just before Gran Tarajal, turn off to the left on a paved road toward Las Playitas (shown on some maps as Las Playas), a pretty little town cut out of cliffs above the sea. Presently, Las Playitas is midway between being a centuries-old core fishing village and a tourist resort. Those of you who know Sausalito, the small town across the Golden Gate Bridge from San Francisco have an idea of what Las Playitas will probably be in ten or twenty years. But not yet. Now it's a remarkably charming place, secluded and quiet.

After walking up and down the beach, we turned up a couple of steep streets into the old part of the village (typically, the tourist development is separate from homes of the locals), admiring the whitewashed houses with flower boxes everywhere—geraniums in the windows, jacandra climbing the patio walls. There were fishing nets out for drying and mending at almost every house.

It didn't take us long to decide that even though it was early, we would have lunch here before heading south, especially since, at that point, dinner was a question mark. We sniffed at the doors of a couple of restaurants and settled on Brisamar, which was built right against the sea, with waves crashing against a breakwater a few feet from our open window.

On the flat part of the beach, a line of overturned fishing boats were basking in the sun. The wind wafted the salty smell of the drying boats to our window, making our sharp white wine and Pulpos taste even better. The tender pieces of octopus were doused with olive oil and sprinkled with salt and paprika. With these we had a plate of fried Pimientos Padron. These two-inch long dark green peppers, found all over the Canaries as well as the Mainland, are one of my favorite tapas. Deep fried, greaseless and sprinkled with coarse salt, one pepper is mild and the next might be a little hot. Always a surprise.

For our main dish we shared a wonderfully fresh and perfectly grilled Rodaballo, or turbot, with a plate of the ever-present and ever-welcome Papas Arrugadas, or wrinkled potatoes, and a simple mixed salad. Later I discovered that upstairs at this restaurant they serve pizza.

After lunch, we continued to head south, exploring on the way. We took a close look at Gran Tarajal, which most guides to Fuerteventura dismiss as a "port city." In fact, there is a fine, long, sand beach which had attracted a crowd of local surfers who rode the waves from Africa as they broke. At the south end of the beach, there is a protected cove with fishing and diving boats for rent.

But the beach of everyone's dreams, the one you always see in the tourist brochures, begins at Tarajelejo and continues south to Morro del Jable, with few interruptions. For most of that distance—just over thirty kilometers—the highway hugs the coast. The road never goes more than one to two kilometers away and the beaches are always visible, with trails leading down to the white sand.

There are few towns between Tarajelejo and Morro, so it's best to pack a picnic if you plan on making a day of it. Bring plenty of sunscreen, because the sun is almost always shining on the Jandia Peninsula. The backbone of this narrow finger of land, poking out into the Atlantic, is an ancient volcanic ridge which has, over the years, grown fatter by catching sand carried on the wind from Africa. So, anyone who has walked on the beaches of Jandia can truthfully claim to have been to 'Africa,' since that's where all the sand came from.

There are a number of outstanding restaurants in the area of Morro and a several good hotels, with more being built all the time. If you are a true beach nut, Morro is probably the best place to base yourself on Fuerteventura. You could have even more fun by renting a jeep or an off-road bike and exploring the many unpaved trails that continue beyond Morro or that climb the mountains to the west and dip down to the virtually unexplored beaches on the northwest coast of the peninsula.

For backpackers, feet could be enough, as the mountains are not steep. At its widest point, the Jandia Peninsula is less than twenty kilometers (thirteen miles) across. And even though the landscape looks like a desert and is a desert, it's temperate. Temperatures rarely cimb over eighty-five degrees and the nights can be chilly, especially in the mountains. Just throw enough food in the pack to cover your trip and, of course, carry plenty of water, because there are few towns on the northwest coast south of La Pared. You can camp anywhere along the coast or in the mountains. A secondary road from Pájara leads to La Pared. Once there, you can see the remains of a stone wall built across the entire peninsula by two Guanche chiefs before the Spanish conquest.

One destination to which you can either hike or ride is the almost empty village of Cofete. A ruined church near the beach is said to have World War II connections with a Nazi espionage ring. There are signs of civilization at Playa de Cofete. There is excellent underwater diving, board surfing, windsurfing, and fishing all along this virtually deserted coast. Fishing and diving boats may be chartered at Morro del Jable for day trips around the tip of the island to the northwest coast.

For those with a botanizing bent, many rare plants grow in the mountains of the Jandia Peninsula, especially around Pico de la Zarra. There is a very rare blue-flowered viper's bugloss that is found nowhere else in the Canaries. A red-flowered spurge, Euphorbia handiensis, which looks like a spiny cactus grows near the coast and is in danger of extinction. But for the amateur botanist, the dune area is probably the most interesting. A great many salt-tolerant species are there, including a yellow-flowered legume, *Lotus lancerottensis*.

If you are lucky, you may get a glimpse of the magnificent Houbara buzzard, a desert-dwelling bird, with a wingspread of over two feet and long black and white display feathers on its neck. In silhouette it looks a bit like a hen turkey.

Fuerteventura is a good place to get lost and maybe find yourself. After a few hours alone on a mountain trail or an empty beach, Unamuno's words come back: "An oasis in the middle of civilization's desert."

## USEFUL INFORMATION

Tourist Office, Avenue Primero de Mayo 33, Puerto del Rosario: 928-85 10 24.

For information about diving and boat charters in the north, contact Barakuda Club Corralejo, Calle José Segura Torres, 20, Correlejo: 928-88 62 43.

For information about diving and boat charters in the south, contact Club Náutico Mar Azul, Puerto Azul, Tarajelejo: 928-87 01 48.

There is also a tourist information desk at the airport.

FUERTEVENTURA

# EL HIERRO

*H*ierro is a roughly triangular island of 107 square miles, the smallest and the most southwestern of the Canaries. About 7500 people live on Hierro, 2000 of them in the capital of Valverde. The highest point on the island is the peak of Malpaso at 4925 feet. The entire island has been constructed on such a steep slope that it appears very possible to trip and fall into the sea at any moment. The airport's runway, which is not long enough for international jets, had to be built on landfill, as there was no area flat enough to contain it otherwise.

Like the rest of the Canaries, Hierro was formed by volcanic action; the entire upper plateau of the island is an ancient volcanic rim and there are extensive ancient lava flows. The island gets less rainfall than Tenerife or Gomera, but the upper pastureland is green because of evaporation from fogs.

Hierro's place in history was assured in the second century A.D. when Claudius Ptolemaeus, or Ptolemy, the Alexandrian astronomer, geographer and mathematician, placed 0 meridian through the island; he believed it to be the westernmost land mass in the world. The meridian stayed there until 1884, when "mean time" was moved to Greenwich.

The Moors raided Hierro for slaves during the thirteenth and fourteenth centuries, which is sometimes said to be why the island's population was so small in 1403 when Juan de Béthencourt landed, fresh from his conquests of Lanzarote and Fuerteventura. Apparently, Béthencourt believed the island to be unpopulated at first. In fact, the aborigines—

called Bimbaches on Hierro—were hiding in the mountains, fearful that the Spanish were slave traders. Finally, the Spanish lured them down.

Well, they should have stayed in the mountains. After the Bimbache chief agreed to peace terms and his 100 or so men put down their arms, they were promptly imprisoned and—yes—sold into slavery. The story goes now that the form of Castilian spoken on Hierro is very pure because there are very few Bimbaches left, only Castilian speakers.

The island was the target of frequent pirate raids right through the eighteenth and early nineteenth centuries, one reason the capital is inland.

## WHERE TO STAY

*H*ierro gets even fewer international tourists than Gomera, even though it has an airport and Gomera does not. But many of the other islanders take short holidays on Hierro for the quiet. Or, as an herreño put it, "they come here to eat and drink and be quiet." And they certainly have the right idea. Imagine a capital city of some 2000 people, white houses strung invitingly up a green canyon above the ocean, where you are just about as likely to meet a goat in the street as a human being. Imagine a capital where the center of social life is the taxi stand across the street from the tourist office.

Hierro is not for everyone, but if you are looking for a few days or weeks of peace, you're on the right island. Where you lay your head at night might be a little perplexing, but there are rooms, pensiones and cottages for rent, as well as a few—very few—hotels. But not to worry—"tranquilo, it will work out." The tourist office in Valverde is helpful, but the best sources of information by far on Hierro are the taxi drivers. The entire Hierro taxi fleet is a co-op and the drivers take a great deal of pride in showing off the island. If there is a vacant room at the world's smallest hotel (the Puntegrande) or a fishing boat for rent in La Restinga, they'll know about it. If you do insist on a hotel room with some pretensions to international standards, it is advisable to book ahead.

## *Camping*

There is one only one offical campsite on Hierro, but backpackers seem to be free to camp anywhere they wish, after asking permission.

# WHAT TO EAT AND DRINK

## *The Food*

Begin with the sea, of course. It is possible to eat in Hierro for at least a week and never eat the same fish twice. There are the standard rockfish, as well as bonita, several kinds of tuna, mackerel, herring, bluefish and delicious mussels. You are likely to find cabrito (goat) on the menu in Hierro, as well as rabbit, lamb and chicken.

Most meals arrive with a selection of mojo sauces, including one that is special to Hierro (though seen occasionally on other islands)—the mojo queso. Another unusual Hierro mojo is a green sauce with an avocado and cilantro base.

Cheese is the real treat on Hierro. It's a blend of cow, sheep and goat milk and is available smoked, or ahumada, aged and firm, curada , or soft and white, blanco. Herreño cheese is exported to the other islands. The curada is the most popular.

There's a local style of quesadilla, with a thicker crust than one normally encounters. It is normally made in a fluted mold, about three inches across. The dish was originally a special food of the Romero (pilgrimage) held every four years to honor the Bajada al Santuario de Nuestra Señora la Virgen de los Reyes, the island's patroness. But the dish became too popular to be confined to the festival and is now sold in bakeries and offered as a tapa in the bars. It is very like the quesadilla of El Salvador.

A sign of the strong Canarian-South American connection is a Venezuelan-style empanada, a popular and quite delicious snack on Hierro. The dough for the crescent-shaped pastry is very similar to the crispy Venezuelan arepa, a corn meal cake made from precooked ground corn. On Hierro, the empanada is made of corn meal, filled with chicken and served with a mojo picante to spoon inside.

## The Wine

"Before the ferry and the planes came, people here had everything they needed. They grew all of their own food, made their own wine. Now everything comes on the ferry. My grandfather is eighty-five. He still has his garden and his wine. He wouldn't think of drinking bottled wine that someone else had made."

—A taxi driver on Hierro

Hierro has some of the best local wines in the Canaries, both table and dessert wines. There is a large cooperative at Tigaday, near Frontera, the Centrale Vinicola Insular, which makes about 250,000 liters of wine a year, mostly white from the Listan grape, but some red from the Listan negra.

The co-op has right up-to-date equipment—more stainless steel wine tanks that we saw anywhere else on the islands—and is even bringing in a few American oak barrels for the red wines. A tasting of the co-op wines showed a wide range of quality, but most of the wines were well-made, decent enough quaffs. A few herreño wines are shipped to the other islands, but as the co-op winemaker Jose Maria Estaben said, it is difficult to compete with wines from the Mainland, not only on price but in quality and consistency. He feels that the quality of the co-op wines will improve with better viticultural practices.

Presently on Hierro, vines are pruned close to the ground, production is low and there are many fungus diseases. Vines are grown on steep, rock-walled terraces, rather than on the gently sloping land near the sea.

The wine cooperative is part of a much larger agricultural cooperative that includes bananas, pineapples, tomatoes and other commercial farm products. It is startling to see wine grapevines and banana trees growing in the same field,

**JOSÉ MARIA ESTEBAN, THE WINEMAKER AT THE CO-OP WINERY ON HIERRO.**

so unusually close to the sea.

The Bimbaches are said to have distilled an alcoholic liquor from laurel berries, which would be quite extraordinary, if true, since the Bimbaches had no metal or glass containers to facilitate distillation. Perhaps there has been some confusion in translating the old texts and the Bimbaches were making a kind of laurel berry beer or wine by a fermentation process. The modern-day product is most often a laurel berry aguardiente. To find the real herreño wine treasures, however, you need to hunt out the small, private cellars.

## *Restaurants*

A surprising number of good restaurants are scattered around the island. The Parador serves the most traditional island food in the typically solemn Parador atmosphere. The choice of white tablecloth restaurants is limited, but dozens of smaller bar-restaurants offer very good food quite cheaply. By all means, have at least one or two meals at the Parador.

The Bar Zabagu at Calle San Francisco 9 in Valverde has wonderful empanadas and is generally good for tapas, lunch or dinner. There are several other good cafés or bars in Valverde. Just follow your nose.

Restaurant Noemi at Las Casitas near Frontera is a remarkably good country-style restaurant. It's perched up on the hillside, overlooking the rocky beach and the tiny hotel, The Puntegrande.

The village of Restinga at the southern tip of the island is crowded with good seafood restaurants. It's expected that you will walk into the kitchen and inspect the fish to be sure that they are fresh and to pick the one you want.

There is also a fair restaurant (designed by César Manrique) in the Mirador de la Peña, where the food is secondary to the sensational views of the coast and the islands of La Palma, Gomera and Tenerife. It's a great place to stop for an afternoon coffee.

## WHAT TO DO

*N*ap. Eat. Take a hike. Nap. Eat. Go wind-surfing. Charter a fishing or diving boat. Nap. Eat. Go looking for a traditional bodega. Take another hike. Memorize a short poem in Spanish. Be still.

Let's be honest here. Any experienced tourist could "do" Hierro before lunch—after a late breakfast. If you are looking for stunning architecture, world-class museums, all-night discos, three-star restaurants, championship golf courses or the like, don't go to Hierro. On the other hand, if you want miles and miles, days and days of good, honest food and drink, peaceful hours spent on mountain trails or exploring a spectacular, rocky coastline, this is the place for you.

Despite some touristic inroads, Hierro is still an island geared to the pace of agriculture and fishing. One keeps an eye on the changes of the seasons, the waxing and waning of the moon, not on digital watches and computer calendars. On a bright, sunny day in January, I noticed that the vineyards were still an untamed tangle of last year's vines.

"Why hasn't the pruning started yet?" I asked.

The answer came back without a trace of self-consciousness. "The moon isn't right."

Ah, pruning by moon signs. No doubt the viticulture department at the University of California, Davis is looking into that. But don't scoff. It could just be true.

The vineyards are on steep, terraced hillsides above the area on the west coast of Hierro known as El Golfo, near the town of Tigaday, which is the wine center of the island. A zig-zag up and down the mountain road leads from Valverde over the central Nisdafe area (the ancient, collapsed volcanic crater) to the spectacular western shore of the island.

Let's say you have chosen the Parador as your Hierro base. A bit inconvenient, since it's a good ten miles from Valverde, even though some guide books call it five miles. Still, on such a small island, it hardly matters. We left the Parador after a late breakfast of excellent espresso, soft cheese and fresh fruit, stopped for a quick orientation at the tourist office in Valverde, took the long way to El Golfo, where we visited the winery co-op in Tigaday and had a tasting, and were still embarrassingly early for lunch.

There was really no excuse for the rush—we simply didn't know what a short drive it was across the island. We had been told the road was bad, which wasn't true. The road is splendidly breathtaking with its hairpin curves and blind corners, but it is actually very well constructed. After all, Hierro has the advantage of having come late to road building, with the first major road (the one eventually leading to the Parador) not built until 1914, so the island isn't saddled with a lot of poorly-designed roads.

Many areas of the island can only be reached by rough tracks that are out of the question for anything except four-wheel drive vehicles, particularly that area known as El Julan, a long, beautiful stretch of coastline on the southwestern shore of Mar de las Calmas, or the calm sea. From a pine forest, a rugged series of weathered volcanic canyons drop in steep cliffs toward the sea. It's a real no man's land, but—at least where it can be approached—it has a rugged beauty somewhat reminiscent of Utah's canyon land country.

There is an unpaved track that roughly (very roughly) follows the coast from El Golfo around the western tip of the island, clinging to the edge of the forest above the badlands of El Julan. This is a day's drive over a road that is beyond bumpy and sometimes narrows to one lane, though the traffic remains two-way. It's a spectacular drive. We would advise taking a hearty picnic (hope you remembered the empanadas), plenty of water and wine and a local driver. There are Bimbache inscriptions at a site called Los Letreros, but the area has been vandalized and is now guarded. You would need a letter from the tourist office to look at the inscriptions.

The track goes past the Ermita Nuestra Señora de los Reyes, the island's patron virgin. According to the story, the statue dates back to 1576-1577 when a French ship was

**EL HIERRO**

becalmed off the coast in the "tranquil" sea. The ship ran out of supplies, but the local people took food to the sailors. The captain had no money to pay for the food, but he gave the islanders the statue of the Virgin Mary from his ship. On that very day, which happened to be January 6, 1577, King's Day (the major feast day of Christmas for the Spanish), a wind came up and the ship sailed away.

That was the first of the Virgin's miracles. She is also credited with ending a severe drought in the eighteenth century. In honor of that climatic miracle, she is taken from her sanctuary once every four years and paraded around the island to Valvedre. This traveling road show begins on May 30 and ends on July 29. During that period, there is extensive feasting, musical events and all sorts of fairs featuring local island crafts. It's a major party. The last outing for the Virgin was in 1989, so June of 1993 would be a good time to visit

Hierro.

Back at El Golfo, across the island from the Virgin's sanctuary, we had an informal tour of what the Guinness Book of World's Records calls the world's smallest hotel, the Puntagrande. The sea was high that day and the tiny four-room hotel is perched like a great stone seabird on a spit of rock jutting out well beyond the rest of the shore  Waves constantly splashed the terrace in front of the hotel and sprayed the window of the snug little bar that overlooked the sea on the hotel's first floor.  The bar and restaurant were closed that day, but an off-duty bartender gave us a quick tour and a peek into one of the rooms.

It's a delightful place.  All done up like a ship, which is quite fitting, since the entire solid stone structure shakes and seems to roll and pitch as each tremendous breaker batters against the rocky outcrop. There was quite by chance a room vacant that day and, looking back, I don't know why we didn't just check in and stay about a month.  In fine weather, it would be marvelous to sit outside on the terrace, having a few bites of fish taken from the sea only about five yards away.  One of life's missed opportunities, I fear.

However, it would have been a pity to have missed the lunch we did have at the Restaurant Noemi, a few hundred yards up the hill from the hotel.  Our taxi driver said it was a good seafood restaurant, but he didn't know if we could get a table, especially since the hotel was closed and the hotel regulars would be sure to go to Noemi.

While we had a glass of the local white wine in the bar, he went into the kitchen to negotiate directly with Noemi, who cooks and serves with the help of a busboy-dishwasher. The discussion dragged on as Noemi, a bustling woman in her mid-forties, tried to calculate the bookings for lunch, while watching over the grill, the oven, the wine orders and incoming traffic. We began to wish we had ordered a liter of the local white or, better yet, a bottle of the Torres Gran Vina Sol we saw behind the bar.

But the delicate discussions couldn't be rushed. Besides,

how could we complain?  There we sat, sipping at a decent enough white wine and looking through the window at a panoramic view of the Atlantic Ocean.  There wasn't a ship in sight.  The local fishermen stay on shore when the wind is high and Hierro is right outside the main shipping lanes; also, most of the trade with the other Canaries is done from the east side of the island nowadays.

At last, the driver returned.  "All right," he said, "we have a table.  It's right by the kitchen door, the worst table in the restaurant, but it's the best I could do."

It turned out to be perfect, because we had a view directly into the kitchen and could watch Noemi in action.  Perhaps not as dramatic as the oceanview tables at the window in front, but watching an experienced  cook in action can also be a theatrical experience.  At a very basic level, food is theater.

There is no printed menu.  Your choice is fish, fish soup or a veal chop, perhaps a pork chop on alternate days.

A plate and three bowls of mojo sauces were set before us with a basket of bread.  One  bowl of sauce turned out to be a special house mojo of tomato, cilantro, garlic, cheese, salt, hot peppers, oil and stock—no vinegar.  The second mojo had avocado and cilantro and the third had sweet red pepper with garlic, oil and vinegar.  All were first rate and we ate them with the bread, the salad, the potatoes and later with the fish.   A mixed salad of lettuce and vegetables was delicious with the cheese mojo.   The Canarians and the Mainland Spanish are particularly fond of the canned white asparagus which were in the salad, but we are not.   The cheese mojo did a lot to enliven their white blandness.

Grilled whole, eight-inch long Cabrilla and fillets of Peto, a forty pound fish like halibut along with Salema, a delicious strongly flavored fish, came with a choice of boiled new potatoes or french fries.   Fresh pineapple completed this excellent lunch.

After lunch, by way of a dessert treat, we drove up the hillside to meet Señor Domingo Morales, one of the last

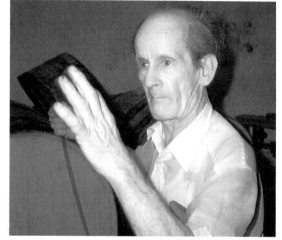

**DOMINGO MORALES, A FIERCLY INDEPENDENT WINEMAKER, IN HIS CELLAR ON HIERRO**

traditional winemakers of Hierro. He was in his mid-seventies. When I shook his gnarled hand, I thought of my grandfather, who had also been a farmer. His hand had that same roughness which comes from working in the earth in all sorts of weather.

Although Señor Morales sells some of his grape crop to the co-op just a few kilometers down the road from his home on Calle Unchons overlooking the Atlantic, he keeps back a good part to make wine for his "family" as he said, with a sly wink.

He led us into his cellar, a small room about ten feet wide by twenty feet long, dug out of the hillside underneath his house. Outside, the low, ground-hugging vines marched almost to the house itself. They were Malvasia, the traditional sweet wine grape of the Canaries. His tiny, cramped cellar was a time machine, whisking the modern visitor straight back to the the time of Sir John Falstaff when the favorite tipple of the English was Canary "sack."

While tasting from the barrels in Señor Morales' cellar, came one of those rare moments of truth: As I held the glass up to the light, looking at the deep amber color, breathing in the smell of the cellar, a heady combination of earth and wine, I realized that this wine was probably very much like the wine of Shakespeare's time. With its bold, intense flavors, the wine would have exactly suited the Elizabethans' taste; they loved highly spiced, strongly flavored foods. Although we now think of these wines as dessert wines, five centuries ago, sweet wines were commonly served with food.

But beyond the obvious flavors of the wine and the way it was made, there was an element which the French would call terroir, which I call "spirit of place," that fixed the wine forever in my palate; it tasted of the Canarian earth, of the dry volcanic soils of the vineyard just a few yards away. It was a strong wine, not only in an alcoholic sense, but also in the sense of enduring. I could almost believe, in the dim cellar, lit only by a single low-wattage bulb, that the wine in my glass was a close cousin of the wine the Elizabethans drank five hundred years before.

Some of the barrels could have been almost that old as well, but they were scrupulously clean. They came in all shapes and sizes, including a very unusual barrel, only about one foot across and about three feet long. It is used to transfer wine from one large barrel to the next, as these wines are made in a solera system like sherry.

In the solera system, wine from the new vintage, let's call it Vintage A, is added to last year's vintage, or Vintage B. Then, some of Vintage B is added to wine from the previous year, Vintage C, and so forth for as many vintages as the winemaker chooses to put in his solera. At least, that is how it works in the traditional dessert wine cellars of the Canaries; the true solera system in Jerez where sherry is made is considerably more complicated than that. But the thrust of the system is to mix different vintages, which tends to smooth out the bad years.

There are a few other traditional winemakers left on Hierro. You won't find any signs directing you to their cellars since these men operate in a kind of legal limbo. The "revenue officers" are not likely to raid them—but, on the other hand, they are expected to keep a low profile. As with everything else on Hierro, the best way to find a traditional bodega is to ask a taxi driver!

A few days later, we met another old-style winemaker, José Panchillo, who lives in the tiny town of Charmoro. We were visiting him, not to see his cellars (that was an unexpected bonus), but to see his chilis. Panchillo is one of those herreños who went to South America as a young man, looking for work. He was successful enough to return to Hierro some thirty years later, buy a home and settle down to cultivating his garden and making a little wine. His "cellar" was above ground and was, in fact, an old garden shed, but in the reasonably cool climate of Hierro, the wine didn't suffer. After we had ritually tasted wine from each of the eight barrels, each one stronger than the one before—Señor Panchillo's solera seemed to concentrate the alcohol wonderfully—we moved on to the chiles, of which he was growing six to eight varieties. Not that he focused solely on chiles. The walled garden behind his house was an organic gardener's paradise. There were heaps of compost in the corners, seashells between the rows ("for the calcium") and everywhere, evidence of a dedicated gardener at work.

Señor Panchillo had traveled and worked throughout South America, from Chile to Venezuela, and wherever he went, he collected chile seeds. Back on Hierro, he grew the chiles and used them in a series of mojo sauces, ranging from mild and tangy to one that is very hot. He took great delight in playing with various combinations, blending and creating new mojos to match particular dishes, almost as if he were creating a wine cuveé.

This adaptability is the great strength of mojo—by

varying the ingredients only slightly, one can create subtle differences in flavor and texture for everything from potatoes to fish to rabbit and goat and maybe even one's fingers and toes. In fact, with his chiles, Señor Panchillo was playing a minor variation on the mojo theme, because chiles are not a major ingredient of mojos—that honor goes to garlic, parsley, cilantro and pimientos. But as in any combination, even the minor elements can effect major changes in the final product, and that was Señor Panchillo's mission with his chilis.

En route back to the Parador, we stopped at the Mirador de la Pena. We ordered an espresso and a glass of brandy and took them to a window with an incredible view. We could see beyond the green forests, beyond the ancient lava flows that spilled past Frontera to the coast, and out into the Atlantic. But it was difficult to decide whether to look at the magnificent view outside or the magnificent views inside. The restaurant was designed by César Manrique and it is perfectly sensational. There is a remarkable blending of stone, wood, tile and glass with lavish use of plants, most

**JOSÉ PANCHILLO MAKES A POINT ABOUT HIS WINE OUTSIDE HIS TINY BACKYARD BODEGA ON HIERRO.**

of them growing from natural stone walls, which form part of the structure of the building itself.

Perhaps the best thing we have "discovered" on the Canaries is the wonderful art of Manrique. He establishes a working relationship with the site, bending the structure to the physical surroundings, so that the building seems to have grown just where it is, an organic part of the land. Manrique uses water—either in pools or fountains—as a kind of gracenote, a means of focus. because water is of such critical importance on all of the islands. The restaurant at the Mirador on Hierro was our first experience with a finished Manrique project, and it was amazing.

. . . . . . . . . . . . . **SNAPSHOT**

*An attractive woman in her mid-thirties parked her expensive Volvo at the edge of a road in the Nisdafe near San Andrés, about ten kilometers from Valverde. She was well-dressed, with an expensive leather bag over her shoulder.*

*She took two five-gallon plastic containers from the trunk of her Volvo and filled them with water from a small pipe set horizontally into the hillside.*

*The water trickled out, filling the containers slowly. This gave me time to decide to be nosy enough to ask her why she came there to get water.*

*"Well, you see, I grew up on a farm just down the road. We always drank this water when I was a child. It suits me. I come up here every few days, just for our drinking water."*

One of the major tourist sights on Hierro is near the village of San Andrés at the spot where a sacred Bimbache tree, the Garoë, once stood. The semi-legendary tree condensed water, forming pools that the Bimbache and the Spanish pioneers used in primitive irrigation projects. The aboriginal inhabitants of Hierro apparently believed the tree had the unique ability to distill water from its leaves, but of course most trees will condense moisture from the atmosphere, releasing it in the form of a steady drip. Some trees are better at this than others. Many Eucalyptuses are extremely efficient. No one knows what variety the original Garoë was, since it was destroyed by a hurricane in the seventeenth century. The present "Garoë" is a lime tree, planted in 1957.

Herreños have also learned to tap into the island's underground water supply—proabably much of that built up by untold centuries of dripping trees—by driving pipes horizontally into the hillsides. These pipes eventually hit water, which begins flowing down the pipes and is captured for irrigation and drinking water.

Stones also condense water, so the small circular stone corrals scattered throughout the high pastureland of Hierro serve a double purpose; they not only contain sheep, but also add to the meager rainfall to help keep the pastures green.

The pasture uplands of Hierro are some of the greenest in the world, watered by almost daily exposure to fog and mist; one gets an eerie displaced feeling, as if one had suddenly been transplanted to the depths of the Irish countryside or the mountains of Wales. The feeling is reinforced by the stone walls, the sheep and goats, the stunted junipers, twisted by the wind into bizarre, witch-like shapes beckoning at the edge of the field, bits of fog caught in the branches. There are windswept reaches of the California coast around Big Sur that have shaped cypress trees in the same fashion.

Dropping down from these green highlands, we returned to the normal world of the Canaries. We passed a thoughtful goat perched on top of a tumbling rock wall, calmly eyeing the taxi as it passed, taking us back to the Parador and an excellent dinner of perhaps that goat's very own cousin, among other delights.

As with most of the Spanish Paradors, the ambience at the Parador Nacional El Hierro is so restful that one could spend hours sitting at the small, tiled bar just off the lobby, sipping a glass of sherry, looking out over the sea and scheming about ways to spend a good part of each year living on Hierro time.

But, alas, even though time may creep at a seemingly pre-industrial pace on Hierro, it does move forward, and soon it was time to dress for dinner. Now, one does not have to dress for dinner in a Parador. There are not actually any dress codes posted, but somehow dining in a Parador has a touch, a shade of Spanish formality about it. This can, at times, lapse into the merely pretentious and one longs for the easy give-and-take of a local tapas bar or country restaurant. However, at best, it is possible to get caught up in the slightly hushed atmosphere, to speak quietly of things that matter—poetry and art, religion and royalty—to study the color of the wine in the excellent crystal on the table and pay careful attention to the food on the plate. In short, to play the part of the pampered guest.

That particular night, we walked into the subdued dining room and were taken to our table. The table was a little low and the chair a trifle high, so as Ann sat down, her knee hit the table, upsetting every glass—and there were many—with a great clash and clatter. Not a head nor an eyebrow in the room moved, and whispered conversation continued as usual. It's called keeping cool in the Parador.

Alfonsiño con ajos y burgados, a small fish, butterflied and baked with garlic slices, a glaze of tomato sauce and a scattering of periwinkles, and roast kid with garlic and parsley in a rich brown sauce helped relieve our embarrassment. We really enjoy the cheese of Hierro, so we choose an excellent, fine textured, smoked cheese, sliced and drizzled with local honey for dessert.

The following morning, we started the day in Valverde, mapping out our schedule at The Bar Zabagu over a plate of fresh-from-the-oven Venezuelan-style empanadas. Our destination was the southern city of Restinga to check out the diving and snorkeling, as well as the freshness of the fish in the many excellent restaurants. First, we wandered around the island's capital a bit, exploring the tower of Nuestra Señora de la Concepciòn, which was built in the mid-eighteenth century as a lookout tower for pirates. The museum next door to the tourist office doesn't take long to see, but has some interesting archaeological exhibits.

An energetic walker can quickly end up right outside Valvedre and halfway to the attractive harbor of Tamaduste, a sheltered rocky cove. Many herreños have second houses here, which some call their "fishing" homes. It isn't unusual to have two homes on Hierro, one in the uplands where goats and sheep are herded for grazing in the summer, the other on the coast to use for fishing and during the grape and fig harvest. This might seem strange on such a small island, but it is a holdover from the roadless days.

En route to Restinga, you pass through the almost overlapping villages of El Pinar, Taibique and Las Casas. The museum in El Pinar, the Museo Panchillo, sells handicrafts, honey and local homemade cheeses. A craft specialty is the talega, a wool bag once worn by herdsmen like a mini-knapsack. The Artesania Ceramica, which sells local pottery, is nearby.

El Pinar, as the name would indicate, is in a large pine wood, a lovely place for a quiet stroll or longer hike with a well-supplied picnic tucked into your talega. There is excellent hiking all over the island. El Pinar lies just at the edge of a dense forest zone, a fog-fed lush upland region of laurel and pine. Almost anyone you ask will be glad to stop and take the time to point out some rough trails you can follow, sometimes even supplying some friendly guidework. More often than not, you will find yourself walking in the hoofprints of centuries of goats, four-footed hikers who seem to prefer trails with good views and plenty of wildflowers. There are some unusual varieties, including a pink-flowered forget-me-not and a pink-flowered campion.

Bird watchers can stay active on Hierro; be on the lookout especially for hawks and other large raptorial birds.

Local guides (in Spanish) to both flowers and birds are available in the tourist office at Valvedre.

Driving south out of El Pinar toward the sea and toward lunch in La Restinga, you leave the pines and green pastureland behind and pass through a zone of volcanic activity where entire mountainsides have been drowned in lava with a few green areas breaking through only here and there.

Restinga itself is in that half-suspended state, poised rather awkwardly between its past life as a small fishing village and its soon-to-be-life as a tourist destination. It isn't doing badly at all for a town that did not even get running water until 1974.

A lot of German and Scandinavian tourists come to Restinga, not for the beach, which is rocky, but for the snorkeling and diving, which is excellent in small scattered coves and pools all along this stretch of coastline. The confirmed beachaholic can find good beaches a little west of Restinga, toward the Bahia de Naos (also good for diving).

The day we left Hierro, we shared a bottle of wine at the airport with the taxi-driver, the guide who had helped us discover Hierro.

We asked him what his plans for the rest of the week were—did he have any more tourists coming in?

"No, not now. I think for the next few days I will go fishing."

Ah, yes, life on Hierro.

It was not a place we wanted to leave.


· · · · · · · · · · · · · · · **SNAPSHOT**

*Just down the road from the Parador at seven in the morning, a small truck pulled off the road. Two men got out, one carrying a stool and a milk pail. The other went out into the shrub and started rounding up goats. Most of the goats were as eager to get to the truck as he was to find them. It was milking time on Hierro, with the milker coming to the goats.*

*Far out over the sea, the sun was breaking through the offshore cloudbank, casting long golden shadows up the eastern-facing canyons, which seemed to be filled with goats. With their voices rising in the early morning air, they were like strange four-footed songbirds, coming down the canyon to greet the sun, and the milkman.*

## Useful Information

Tourist Information, Valverde: 922-80 54 80.

# EL HIERRO

88

omera is an almost round island of just under 150 square miles. About 18,000 people live on the island, one-third of those in the capital, San Sebastian. The highest point on the island is the Alto de Garajonay (in the national park of the same name) at just under 5000 feet. The Roman Pliny called Gomera "Junonia Minor" and the nearby island of La Palmas, "Junia Mayor."

Like the rest of the Canaries, Gomera dropped off the maps for over a thousand years, but popped up in 1382 when a storm drove a Galacian sailor named Castro onto the island.

Castro must have had a priest with him, because he baptized the Guanche overlord of the island, renaming him Castro. However, the Galacians didn't establish full-time residence on the island, soon flitting back to the Mainland like any modern tourist group. It wasn't until 1405 that Juan de Béthencourt tried to conquer Gomera for the King of Castile. After rolling over Lanzarote, Fuereventura and Hierro, he no doubt expected an easy conquest. He was wrong. He fought several battles with the Guanches, but finally gave up with the island half-conquered and returned to his native Normandy in 1420. A permanent Castilian governor was sent to Gomera in 1442, but the Guanches weren't completely conquered until a few years before Columbus sailed to the New World, with one bloody uprising as late as 1488.

About 15,000 people a year visit Gomera, compared with two million on Tenerife. Gomera is not really geared up for any major tourist business, which is one of the nice things about the island. Tourism has affected only the capital. The outsider may not notice, but Gomereans are quite concerned about the number of islanders who leave Gomera to work tourist jobs on Tenerife. Life on the farms of Gomera is hard. More than that, a skilled waiter might make as much in one month on Tenerife as he would in a year on a Gomerean farm.

## WHAT TO DO

Gomera, like its sister island Hierro is not for the hyperactive. It's a good place to be lazy and do nothing. To eat and drink too much and practice the Spanish art of the siesta. But if you must be up and going, there are superb hiking trails, both deep sea and coast fishing, swimming, diving, bicycling and botanizing.

## WHERE TO STAY

Only the Parador in San Sebastian and Hotel Tecina in Playa Santiago will suit your needs if you must have international hotel accommodations. On the other hand, there are plenty of inexpensive one- and two-star hotels in San Sebastian. Outside the capital, you must look for pensiones. They are usually much cheaper and often very pleasant, but be sure to inspect the room before striking a deal. You may also find rooms in private homes.

## WHAT TO EAT AND DRINK

The best restaurant on the island is in the Parador; it is also the most expensive. There are dozens of small bar-restaurants in San Sebastian, most specializing in fresh fish. In the country, you are more likely to find goat, lamb, rabbit and game birds, although there will be fish as well. The country-style restaurants all have sound food and little to distinguish them from each other.

A typical country restaurant is La Romantica, on the hillside above Vallehermoso on the road toward Arure. There is a beautiful view of the valley, and good local food such as fried kid, roast lamb and grilled rabbit. The name comes not from any kissy-face, huggy-bear stuff in dark booths, but from regular performances of Gomerean folk singing and dancing, known as "romances."

All of the islands offer gofio—that toasted, ground cereal made of toasted maize, wheat or barley. On Gomera it is not a novelty, but part of the daily diet. The basis of gofio is a staple of the Guanche kitchen. The grain (the Guanches always used barley, which they cultivated) is first toasted, then ground to a consistency rather like that of rough corn meal. It is used as a substitute for bread, added to soups, rolled with honey and nuts for a snack food or used in dozens of other ways.

Yam and sweet potato dishes are common on Gomera, more than on the other islands. Yam and watercress stew is a delicious Gomerean specialty.

There are several varieties of mojo on the island. Standard versions are the mojo picón and the mojo verde.

Gomera has delicious honey and country restaurants often keep their own bees. Palm honey, *miel pomera*, is made from the sap of palm trees, which are "tapped" like maple trees. It's quite tasty.

## *Wine*

A local drink called guarapo is distilled from the palm tree. But there is not much in the way of commercial wine production on Gomera and what the island does have is all white. In fact, at least one of the standard Spanish wine guides completely ignores any wine production on Gomera. It is certainly not easy to find bottled Gomerean wines, although the Parador does offer a pleasant enough *vino de mesa blanco* from Don Salvador. The best way to taste Gomerean wine is to buy the *vino de pais*, or wine of the countryside, at local shops or bars. You will often be directed to someone's garage and will be expected to bring your own container. These wines are certainly worth sampling and some of the dessert wines are quite good, made very much as they must have been almost 500 years ago. For good table wines, the wines of Mainland Spain are available everywhere and are usually cheaper than the local wines that can be found.

The vines are terraced on steep hillsides and grow low and sprawling, yielding very small amounts of grapes. The chief grape is a variety of Palomino (the grape of Spain's sherry district) called Listan in the Canaries.

· · · · · · · · · · · · · **SNAPSHOT**

*We had spent the morning caught in the kind of trap that travel writers should be adept at avoiding: a guide carried away by civic pride had taken us on a tour of a new community center. It was a very nice building, well designed and clearly a structure that the town of Valle Gran Rey could view with pride. But, as we gently reminded our host, it really wouldn't play very well in San Francisco or London. At any rate, we finally broke away and demanded to be taken directly to Arure. We had been told that a restaurant there had wonderful and abundant Gomerean country food.*

*The guide, a very personable native of Gomera named Salvador Borges, smiled the particular smile that signals that a point has been scored and said, "Ah yes, that's where I had planned to take you to lunch. A superb restaurant there called La Conchita. We are lunching there with the mayor and some other old friends."*

*Score one for Señor Borges.*

*The Restaurant La Conchita is just outside Arure and is impossible to miss. It looks a bit like a truckstop café somewhere in Colorado or Extramadura, but once you go inside, you can indulge in hours of pleasurable eating. Ricardo Barroso owns it with his wife, Conchita, who is also the cook. It is filled with a bizarre combination of local farmers and German students eating cheaply, often with a few kids, who are banging plates and calling for more.*

We started with cookies and sweet local dessert wine. A great way to begin lunch! The cookies, called alfajoras, were a variation on an Andalucian cookie, but certainly showed their Arab origins. They were made of honey, almonds, cinnamon and a little flour, baked moist and coated with powdered sugar. Truly delightful. They were followed by a sharp, acidic, local white wine (not in bottles, of course) and a pan con cebolla— more of an onion bagel than a bread— baked that morning in the kitchen and served with a slightly smoked, local goat cheese. Perfect with the wine.

At about this point, our driver joined us for lunch as well as Esteban Bethencourt, the mayor of Valle Gran Rey, and his deputy mayor. The conversation turned to airports and quickly developed into a heated but polite debate over the advantages or disadvantages of an airport for Gomera. One got the feeling it would not have been quite so polite if the American journalists had not been present.

But, just in time, more food arrived and the debate was put aside in favor of a true Gomerean specialty. Small, separate bowls of gofia, ground almonds, honey and smoked goat cheese cut into bite-sized squares were placed on the table. You dip the cheese into the honey, then into the gofia and the ground almonds and pop it straight into your mouth—a heavenly bite, combining crunch, sweetness and creaminess, as well as an exotic smoky flavor from the cheese.

By this time, several bottles of wine from the Mainland were on the table of wine, as well as carafes of local wine— most slightly sweet. I was happy to see our driver taking a moderate approach to the wine, considering the twisting roads of Gomera.

We ate for some time. The food ranged from a delicious

*potato and watercress soup thickened with gofio (which stayed on the table throughout the meal), kernels of corn, white beans, the ubiquitous papas arrugadas served with two different mojo sauces, fresh salad, and two kinds of fish. One was a madegral, a local fish similar to a sea bass. We ate it fried with a picante mojo. There was also a local tuna served in a light tomato and onion sauce like the Catalan sofrito with green peppers.*

*The lunch ended as it had begun, with a sweet—leché al horno, or milk from the oven. It's a first cousin to a flan. After it comes from the oven, a little lemon and honey are poured over the top. It is then cut into squares and served with a local dessert wine.*

*After lunch we walked across the road with Señor Barroso, puffing on our cigars and looking over the green hillside dotted with goats. We were on the main cross-island highway of Gomera, but sometimes five minutes elapsed between cars.*

*I told him how much we had enjoyed our lunch, not only the food and wine, but also the conversation. He nodded, took a long puff on his cigar, then waved it in a brief semi-circle:*

*"Here, we have all we need. We have the land. It is enough. But come back now for coffee and I believe I have another jug of wine from my grandfather's cellar from before the war. I'd like you to try it."*

*It was a little while before I realized Señor Barroso meant the Spanish Civil War.*

The only way to get to the island of Gomera is by sea, which is probably the way one should approach all islands, but especially Gomera with its spectacular rocky cliffs and hidden beaches. At sea level, the island grows gradually on the horizon, like a magnificent, if somewhat irregularly shaped green ship, slowly filling the entire field of vision. Gomera's jumbled, mountain greenery tumbles in a series of steep canyons to the sea, often ending in sheer, rocky cliffs or tiny black-sand beaches, inaccessible except by boat.

**LA GOMERA**

Ignore the city of San Sebastian, where the ferry docks, and the island will probably look very much as it did in 1492, when Christopher Columbus stopped to obtain on water on either his first or second voyage to America (the records aren't precise).

The ferry runs from the port of Los Cristianos at Playa Américas on Tenerife to San Sebastian and back again three times daily. To come to Gomera from Tenerife takes about ninety minutes. Long enough to have a glass of wine at one of the two bars on the ship, or perhaps a quick nap in a comfortable overstuffed chair in one of the saloons. If it is a clear day, relax in a deck chair and catch the marvelous views of Mt. Teide behind you on Tenerife and the cliffs of Gomera ahead.

The coming and going of the ferry sets the pace of the day in San Sebastian and, in fact, for all the island, because the local bus service is tied to the arrival and departure of the ferries.

Most people who come to Gomera are day trippers from Tenerife. Avoid that mistake. Gomera is worth a longer visit. After getting off the ferry, take a taxi directly to the Parador Conde de la Gomera. It's a real jewel in Spain's Parador system. Built in the Canarian colonial style, it looks as if it has stood on its cliff above the bay for centuries, but the doors opened only in 1976! The interior features dark wood and tile, with carefully selected antique furnishings from the other islands and from Mainland Spain.

Overlooking the harbor and the capital, the Parador affords a magnificent view of Tenerife, only about twenty miles away. From a charming sitting room called the Salon de Teide, one can gaze at Tenerife's Mt. Teide. A very pleasant spot to take coffee in the morning with a tumbler of the Venezuelan rum which is a very popular breakfast drink on the island, or to sit in the late afternoon over a glass of the local dessert wine, while looking down at the gulls soaring above the bay.

A terraced garden with many varieties of Canarian plants leads down to the pool and to an informal luncheon site, again, with a fine view of the bay.

Once you have stretched your legs in the garden and admired the view, stop by the tiny bar just off the central patio, a feature of most colonial-style Canarian buildings. Take a glass of chilled sherry or wine or perhaps a café leché (coffee with milk) to one of the many outside tables and let the peace and quiet of the garden-patio soothe your travel-weary spirit. Soon enough, it will be time to be on the move again, because, contrary to what most of the guidebooks say, there is plenty to see on Gomera.

And we may well begin with San Sebastian itself. At first sight, the town looks a bit of a dud, frankly. It doesn't look as if it dates back to the 1400s, but, in fact, it does and was the last scrap of European civilization west of Europe at the time Columbus sailed to the Americas.

Local legend has it that Columbus was interested in more

than refilling his ships' water supplies when he stopped at San Sebastian. The historical gossip is that Donna Beatriz de Bobadilla, a young, attractive and sexually willing widow, was also a prime attraction for the exploring sailor. Four years before, as Donna Beatriz's husband was on his way to visit a Guanche princess, a jealous Guanche chief slew him. Beatriz fled to the Torre del Conde and was living there at the time of Columbus' visited. The tower still stands today, but is not open to the public. It was built around 1450 as a defensive strongpoint against attacks by the Guanches, who had a difficult time, apparently, adjusting to Spanish rule.

Columbus is said to have spent most of his time on Gomera in the tower with Beatriz, but It is possible to visit several other sites associated with Columbus, all of them on the Calle del Medio, the main street of the town. On the corner of the Plaza Constitution is a small, one-story, stone building with a tile roof. There are no records of the house before the seventeenth century, but according to local legend, Columbus took water from a well in the house's patio. A few doors away at 64 Calle del Medio is the Church of the Assumption, where Columbus is believed to have heard Mass before he sailed. Only the facade and the triumphal arch remain of the church of Columbus' time, which was destroyed by Algerian pirates in 1617. The style is predominantly Gothic, although there is a section of fine Moorish or Mudejar ceiling over part of the church. There are also interesting pillars of native red sandstone.

A little further up the calle is the Casa de Colón, a house Columbus ordered to be built between his first and second voyages to America. It's an unremarkable L-shape structure; the design is colonial Canarian known locally as "folk." The house was in private hands until 1966, when the local council purchased it. Now, it is used for art exhibits, small musical events and the like and also houses the local tourist office. Even if you have no interest in Columbus, it's worth a visit to Casa de Colón to check out the current art exhibit. There are some very good painters on Gomera—not heard of, of course, off the island—who well deserve a close look.

Columbus' stopover, for whatever reason, proved to be a stroke of luck for Gomera. Several other explorers followed him, including such notable ones as Amerigo Vespucci, Vasco de Gama and Francisco Pizarro. All spent some time on the island. None others are said to have enjoyed the favors of Donna Beatriz, although she was not known for her discrimination. Gomera's importance in the early discoveries and development of the Americas may owe as much to the charming Beatriz as to the well of sweet water.

If you've had enough of Columbus, there are a number of pleasant bars and small restaurants up and down the Calle del Medio. They are especially inviting in the evenings, with light from inner courtyards splashing out onto the street. Also, in the evening, the streets will be less crowded, since the day trippers will have returned to Tenerife, leaving you to meet some of the locals and perhaps to enjoy a snack of fried sardines before returning to a serious dinner at the Parador.

The kitchen at the Parador on Gomera is very good indeed. In itself, it's worth an overnight visit to the island. Like Paradors all over Spain, one of its culinary goals is to preserve and promote local dishes. Of course, many of the "local" dishes of Spain have spread throughout the country—even as far as the Canaries. A typical Canarian menu, however, might be the one we enjoyed on our first night in Gomera.

Dinner began with three starters. First, dates filled with soft cheese and wrapped in bacon. A delicious combination. The dates were from the Parador's own garden, the cheese from a local goat. There was another cheese appetizer, or tapa, a cheese croquette, also made from local cheese. Two different, thinly sliced hams were served with bread; the famous Iberico ham from the black pigs of Extramadura on the Mainland and an island specialty which they call panchetta—not at all like the Italian meat—made from cured sidepork.

The first course was the Canarian specialty, sopa de puerros, a soup made of potatoes, leeks and salt cod. It is not puréed and has the consistency of porridge. Sometimes garbanzo beans are added. Accompanying the soup was a tarta de cebolla almendra, or onion and clam tart, topped with melted local cheese and sautéed onions. This island specialty was absolutely delicious; its crust was magnificent.

For one main course, we had a local fish called a madegral, similar to a sea bass. It had been broiled and tossed with a picante mojo sauce made of onions, garlic, red pepper, vinegar and a bit of olive oil, but was not at all oily. The mojos on Gomera were outstanding, with a wide range of subtle flavors. The same fish was offered a la plancha (grilled) with the mojo on the side. With the fish came the inevitable but always welcome papas arrugadas. Here, as elsewhere, we ate the tasty little potatoes as finger foods, dipping them into a red mojo sauce. Our other main course was codorniz ciruela, quail with prunes, served in a brown sauce.

For dessert there was date ice cream and a wonderful empanada de manzania de queso, or apple pie with cheese in plain American English, though the pie was anything but a plain American pie. It was about one-inch thick and the bottom and top crust were made with a sharp local cheese. The apple filling had a creamy consistency that went perfectly with the cheese.

There was an extensive selection of wines from the Penedes and Rioja regions of Mainland Spain. We settled on a Torres Viña Sol for starters and followed that with a Torres Gran Coronas. Both wines were excellent complements to the food. The Parador has sought out some local Gomerean dessert wines for the list, which we also sampled. They were quite delicious.

It was a superb meal that presented Gomerean fare in a special setting, but it isn't necessary to go to white tablecloth restaurants to enjoy the bounty of Gomera. There are dozens of small, country restaurants that offer many of the same dishes as the Parador, but perhaps in a more rough-and-ready (and considerably cheaper) setting.

After a sound night's sleep in a television-free environment (right, no TVs in the Parador, but a good international selection of books in the library, should you have neglected to bring your own) it's time to get out to see a little more of Gomera. Be sure you have plenty of film, because once you get a few kilometers outside San Sebastian, the scenery is incredible. If you really pushed it, it would be possible to "do" the rest of Gomera in a day's hard driving. But it wouldn't be much fun. You can do a fairly basic two-day tour that will still give you time for leisurely Spanish-style lunches and another night at the Parador to boot.

The best plan for touring Gomera is to rent a taxi for the day if your budget permits. Ask at the hotel desk and they'll be sure you get a fair deal. However, there are several auto rental agencies down by the harbor and rental rates are much lower in the islands than on the Mainland. There is bus service from San Sebastian to Vallehermoso, Playa Santiago and Valle Gran Rey, but the schedules are designed to get workers into the capital, not tourists out to the countryside. However, it would be perfectly feasible, for example, to take the noon bus from San Sebastian to Vallehermoso, find a room for the night, walk around that lovely little town and take the 9 a.m. bus back to San Sebastian the following day.

Whatever your mode of transportation, one of the first destinations should be the Parque Nacional de Garajonay. Begin at the park visitor's center at Juego de Boplas on the north edge of the park near Vallehermoso, a little over an hour's drive from San Sebastian on a twisting, narrow two-lane highway (but then virtually all the highways on Gomera meet that description). The visitor's center has a reliable map that indicates trails and roads which require four-wheel drive car. In addition, the center offers a display of the park's flora and fauna.

The park covers about ten percent of the island, most of which seems, to be the highest ten percent. It's an amazing experience to drive into the forest. Most days, there's a thick cloud cover, visible from below. As you get closer to the park, little patches of the cover escape, drifting down the steep barrancos, or canyons, sometimes seemingly catching in the tree tops. If you are driving, be very cautious on the park roads. If the cloud cover is low enough, visibility may be only a few yards.

With all that moisture blowing around, the park is a lush green, perhaps the most well-watered area in all of the Canaries. There are a number of fern species, laurel, an indigenous Canarian willow, Canary broom, cistus and heather. The Garajonay is a surviving remnant of the ancient continent-wide *laurisilva* and cedar forest that once covered much of the subtropical world. In 1986, the United Nations declared the entire Garajonay a Heritage of Mankind Park.

Do get out of your car and take at least a short walk through the Garajonay. Within a hundred yards you will have entered another time zone; the silence is dense, complete; the world is a wash of green and gray with perhaps an occasional shaft of sunlight breaking through to highlight a twisted willow trunk or the deep green of a holly bush.

There is a campground within the park, Campamento Antiguo, and another at El Cedro, just outside the park. As almost anywhere in Spain, it is possible to set up a tent in the campo, or countryside, if you ask the owner's permission. Finding the owner on Gomera can be a problem; there's the added difficulty of finding a flat space large enough to hold even a small tent.

The park takes is name from an old Gomerean folktale. A beautiful Guanche girl named Gara was in love with Jonay, a Guanche boy from Tenerife who used to swim across the sea to visit her. Her family was opposed to her marrying the outsider, so Gara and Jonay fled to the top of the mountain and fell onto a huge thorn, dying in each other's arms.

After that story, it must be time for a glass of wine and a bite of food. Luckily, both can be found in the small town of Vallehermoso, only a few minutes away. The town is situated a few kilometers from the sea, nestled in a beautiful but very steep valley, with row upon row of terraced grapevines and banana trees winding hundreds of yards up the hillside. The bananas have been planted closer to the road, because they are heavier to haul out at harvest time than the grapes. Although there is large-scale commercial banana production on Gomera—notably by the Olsen family around Playa de Santiago in Benchijigua valley—in this area, one family may own only a few trees, selling the fruit to the local co-op. Since most of these growers can't afford to buy trucks, the stalks of bananas are harvested, tagged and left by the roadside for pickup by the co-op trucks. The system seems to work fine. Apparently, no one ever tags another producer's bananas. Still, it's a bit disconcerting to drive along the road, seeing stacks of green bananas waiting for pickup.

But there are even more startling sights ahead. Just at the edge of Vallehermoso there is a children's park with a remarkable sculpture group. Three huge figures are seated around a giant table, with two other figures seated on a bench nearby. These concrete figures are at least ten feet high and are meant as a kind of giant toy for children, who are encouraged to crawl over them, use them as a base for various games or to create whatever young minds can. Two of the figures have name tags—Mama and Papa. When I first saw the figures, It seemed a surprising bit of whimsy for what appears to be a practical, little, agricultural town.

Later, we learned that there was definitely a free spirit loose in Vallehermoso. Several years ago, the town cajoled the government in Madrid and obtained money to build a dam in the canyon above, where one of the few year-round streams on the island flows. It cost about US$1 million, which may not be much of a dam by U.S. standards, but it's pretty impressive on Gomera. The dam created a rather small, algae-clouded lake, which is not a must-see in anyone's guide book, but there are two sculptures on the lake shore that for sheer whimsy are worth a look. The first is an oversized concrete fisherman (surely, a work by the same artist who did

**MIGUEL BRITO, THE EX-MAYOR OF VALLEHERMOSO.**

the playground sculptures) holding a real fishing rod; the second is a massive piece of work that initially appears to be an abstract "junk" construction of concrete and metal. What it is, however, is a sculpture created from the concrete mixers used in building the dam.

The wonderful thing about the Spanish sense of humor (which has immigrated to the Canaries in fine shape) is that the people of Vallehermoso show these sculptures off to visiting dignitaries with a completely straight face. It's only when the French agricultural attaché (or whoever) is safely on the way back to San Sebastian that the locals get together in the Bar Central for a glass of wine and a good chuckle.

The second day on Gomera can be a bit more leisurely, but there's still plenty to do. If you have returned to San Sebastian the night before, there is a certain amount of backtracking necessary, as the island's road system is not very extensive. The first stop should be the small village of Chipude. This is about forty-five minutes from San Sebastian, when driving to Valle Gran Rey on the island's west coast. When you arrive in Chipude, it will be about time for a second cup of coffee and a visit to one of several pottery shops that line the main (and only) street. Pottery is still made by very ancient methods—all by hand without wheels and without even a carefully sealed modern oven or pottery kiln.

A few kilometers down the road is the tiny hamlet of El Cercado, also a pottery village. Delia Niebla is one of the young potters of El Cercado who is keeping alive the ancient techniques, which the Spanish learned centuries ago from the Guanches. She learned from her parents, who have a pottery shop on the coast at Valle Gran Rey. Her pottery, like most on Gomera and in the rest of the Canaries as well, is unpainted, of a very simple, appealing design, with a light glaze on most pieces. She has modeled many of her pieces on Guanche kitchen pottery, although she makes hers for decorative purposes.

One unusual design features a pot with holes the size of a quarter in the bottom. It fits into another clay dish, shaped a bit like a planter drain dish. The bottom dish is filled with live coals and the pot is set into the coals. Used at the table, this device serves as a warmer for papas arrugadas, the potato dish that accompanies almost every meal on Gomera.

The day we were in El Cercado was rainy and blustery. There were no other tourists about, so Niebla took us across the highway and a few yards down the hillside to her kiln, which is a simple stone structure, roughly sealed. She fires her pots with brush gathered from the hillside, in exactly the same way the Guanches did thousands of years before. The clay is of a reddish-brown cast and is quite abundant locally, which is why potters settled in the area.

The work of Niebla and the other young potters of Gomera is one of the positive aspects of tourism, because it enables the young people of the island to keep in touch with their historic and cultural roots, while offering a real product that cannot be duplicated anywhere else in the world.

A word of caution: if you buy any of the local pottery, be sure it is well-wrapped for the trip home. Because these pots are not commercially fired at very high temperatures, they tend to break easily.

Tourism has also been responsible for the revival of the tajaraste, or drum dance. The dance is set to the music of a very primitive drum played with a single stick and large castanets, called chácaras. The dance is unlike that on any other island and probably comes from Guanche dance rhythms.

Certainly one of the most fascinating Guanche cultural survivals on Gomera is the whistling language or *silbo gomero*. We were given a demonstration of this amazing form of communication in the garden of the Parador, only hours after our arrival on the island. We had heard of the whistling language before coming to Gomera, but had supposed it to be a crude affair of basic signals, a kind of "where are you?", "here I am" system of keeping in touch over the rugged Gomerean hillsides. The *silbo* language goes far beyond that. Expert whistlers can use the language to give quite complex commands and to ask and answer complicated questions. As an example, one of the Parador gardeners walked several hundred yards away and completely out of sight around a corner of the Parador, while the other stayed with us. We asked questions like: "What will you have for dinner tonight? When did your mother-in-law last visit you?" He answered all the questions. We gave a series of commands that could not possibly have been rehearsed: "Pick a flower and bring it back to us. Put it in Señora Walker's purse." He carried out that command and several others without delay.

Later, we heard (and saw) other demonstrations of *silbo*, including the less piercing indoor whistling and a kind of crooning lullaby whistling that mothers use with babies. Even though men often use the language in the fields, mothers teach it to their children. Actual communication seems to be a matter of both modulating tone and pitch and following the syllabic construction of the words.

At one time, all Gomereans would have learned the whistling language, but that is no longer true. With the few exceptions of those who live in very remote areas, *silbo* survives only as a tourist curiosity.

There are several theories about its origin. One obvious explanation is that a strong whistler can be heard up to four kilometers away, which makes it a useful form of communication on Gomera, where rugged ravines cut through the fields every few hundred yards, making even visual communication impossible. As recently as a few decades ago, *silbo* would be used to summon medical help or exchange other vital news. However, this theory doesn't explain the development of the soft, indoor language.

Some believe that the whistling language was developed by prisoners who had had tongues cut out, and were then dumped on the island by Romans or Arabs. But anyone who has tried to whistle without using the tongue will realize that this theory is nonsense.

Whatever its origin, the whistling language is fascinating and any visit to Gomera should include at least one demonstration. If you stay at the parador, ask at the desk. Otherwise, almost any taxi driver or bartender can arrange it.

Back on the highway and a few kilometers beyond El Cercado, one comes to Valle Gran Rey. The town is perched in a narrow canyon above a yellow-sand beach, which is good for swimming, as it is usually very calm.

Valle Gran Rey is the international zone on Gomera, with hundreds of Europeans, most of them students or at least of student age, living in rented houses or, in some cases, building their own. This Mainland community has a decidedly environmental inclination and has encouraged the native environmentalists in their fight against building an airport on the island.

This is a good area for hiking or bicycling and it is possible to rent bikes at the beach. Most of the students have brought their own.

Valle Gran Rey has several tiny satellite villages including La Calera, a lovely, flower-filled village with enough boutiques for an hour's shopping. You can buy the palm honey and the guarapo liqueur here. Down on the beach are the villages of La Playa Calera and Vueltas. La Playa Calera caters to tourists, Vuyeltas to fishermen. You can also catch a motorboat there called "The Alcatraz," which will take you back to San Sebastian by sea.

It is possible to rent a boat with a skipper here for fishing or simply for playing around on one of the many island beaches that can only be reached by sea. As with most other things on Gomera, there is no commercial office set up for boat rentals. One must walk up and down the dock and ask. However, there is a sailing club in San Sebastian: The Club Nautique: 922-87 10 53. We had heard that they maintain a list of rental boats, but when we asked, no one could find the list. Maybe you'll have better luck.

As you leave the Valle Gran Rey area and head toward the village of Arure, stop at the Mirador de Palmarejo, about eight kilometers above the sea. César Manrique designed the building. Like much of his work, it combines high-tech design principles with a wonderful touch of fantasy.

The site is spectacular. The concrete and glass building, which combines a small restaurant, an art gallery, a museum and a shop, wraps around a solid rock cliff face, with a sheer drop into the valley below. The cliff itself is part of the building's interior wall, with plants still growing out of the rock. Every effort has been made to keep the Mirador as natural as possible. When we were there, it was still under construction, and the workers were taking elaborate precautions to protect the existing plants. They put other native plants into place, even as construction progressed, so the newly-planted specimens would be mature when the building was ready for the public.

. . . . . . . . . . . . **SNAPSHOT**

*I was at my usual table on the Plaza Constitution in Vallehermoso, sipping a glass of wine and enjoying the view, the clean air and that feeling to which one is privileged perhaps once a month that says "all is well with the world."*

I had watched a young woman laboring up the long winding hill toward the Plaza on her mountain bike. She was well-weighted down, I thought, with a sleeping bag and a few other bits of baggage.

She asked if I knew of a room for the night, taking me perhaps for a local. When I heard her Spanish, I tried English, which she spoke perfectly, as do most young Germans, which she was. I directed her to a house up the street where I had seen a "room for rent" sign out earlier in the day. Then I asked her if she had rented the bicycle on Gomera.

"No, I brought it from Germany. I'm only here for a holiday, but I am going to go home, get my boyfriend and come back and stay."

"What will you do?"

"I'm not sure. But I think it doesn't matter."

"But you must live!"

"We will find ways." She shook her head. "Don't you see? This island is so beautiful, so tranquil and peaceful. I am almost thirty years old. All my life I have heard, 'Do this, do that, do well in school, do well in your career.' No one ever told me to look for beauty. Now I've found it. I won't let it go."

## *Useful Information*

For bus and taxi information: 922-80 54 80.
Tourist Office: 922-87 01 03.

# GRAN CANARIA

*G*ran Canaria is shaped a bit like a scallop, which is fitting, since in the middle ages the scallop was a symbol of pilgrims who went on long journeys to see strange, marvelous places and to visit holy shrines. Gran Canaria is a shrine to the modern pilgrim, the tourist. There are about 700,000 permanent inhabitants, with over half of those living in the urban area of Las Palmas, which was founded in 1478. It's the third largest of the Canary Islands—after Tenerife and Fuerteventura—and has by far more visitors than the rest of the islands combined. About 2.3 million people visit Gran Canaria's 592 square miles every year.

The first thought is, oh no, it must be packed with tourists. Well, yes and no. The southern beaches are heavily used, there's no denying that. One seventeen kilometer stretch of lovely white-sand beach centered around Playa de Maspalomas in the south caters almost exclusively to tourists—pubs, bars, restaurants, hotels, marinas, swimming pools, tennis courts, casinos. Whatever you want, it's there.

On the other hand, there are over 200 kilometers of coast on Gran Canaria and much of it has rarely seen a tourist. Inland, Gran Canaria is spectacularly beautiful and, should you tire of gazing at well-tanned bodies on the beach, you can lose yourself on mountain trails and steep green canyons. The capital, Las Palmas de Gran Canaria, is one of the busiest ports in Spain and is a thoroughly modern city with good museums, theater and outstanding restaurants. In short, there is every activity imaginable on the island, from sand and sun to hiking to nightlife in the big city.

Given the natural beauty and bounty of the island, it is no wonder that the Guanches put up such strong resistance to the Spanish on Gran Canaria. The conquest began in 1477, but the final Guanche surrender didn't come until 1483 when, in a dramatic moment, the last two Guanche chiefs lay down their arms, then embraced and leaped over the cliff to their deaths in the sea. Their wives then joined hands and leaped after them.

The recorded history of Gran Canaria goes back much further than that. There is evidence that the Phoenicians had visited the island by the twelfth century B.C. The Carthagian, Hanno, was there in the fourth century B.C. Maps going back to the tenth century after Christ show the island in recognizable form. Portugal claimed Gran Canaria (and the rest of the archipelago) in 1341, but was never able to enforce its claims.

After the Spanish conquest, Gran Canaria followed the typical development pattern of the islands. Agriculture dominated the economic life until the mid-1950s, when tourism began with a small trickle of British and Scandinavians. It's easy to see what brought the tourists—more than 350 sunny days a year or about 3000 hours of sunshine annually.

The island is situated at about mid-point in the Canarian chain. The southern part of the island is close enough to Africa to be influenced by its Saharan winds and climate. But the mountains in the interior, northern part of the island are high enough to attract moisture from the trade winds. So the island follows the Canarian pattern of a dry, almost-desert like south and a more temperate, green north.

## BEING THERE

*T*here is so much to see on Gran Canaria that renting a car is essential. Car rentals are inexpensive, at about one-half the rate of continental Europe and comparable, when we were last there in 1991, to rates in the US. Gasoline is also cheaper than on the Peninsula, but higher than in the US. Most of the island's roads are in good condition, so a four-wheel drive vehicle is rarely a necessity, although one of the open-top jeeps available could be fun. Mopeds and motorbikes are also for rent at most of the large hotels.

The bus system is good on the island and, if you are exploring the capital of Las Palmas or the beach area around Maspalomas, buses are a reasonable alternative to your rental car because of heavy traffic. There is also a nifty little electric train called the Maspalomas Express, which hits the main stops of the tourist beach area.

## WHAT TO DO

*I*t would be easier to describe what isn't available that what is. Let's begin with the beach and the sea. There's every kind of water sport imaginable: sailing, windsurfing, board surfing, water-skiing, underwater diving, fishing, yachting. Once out of the water, there's tennis, golf, hiking, botanizing, birdwatching, bicycling, horseback riding, parachuting—there's even a go-cart track. For spectator sports, there's horse and dog racing, basketball, and soccer.

There are many museums and art galleries, jazz clubs, a philharmonic orchestra, and an opera festival.

Check for phone numbers in the "Useful Information" section.

## WHERE TO STAY

*T*here are tourist class hotels almost everywhere on the island, as well as hundreds of small pensione-type hotels, especially in Las Palmas. Only in January and February are the hotels booked at anything near full capacity. It is perfectly feasible, if you plan on a long visit, to book a hotel only for your first one or two nights, then to find another one or an apartment if you wish.

There are thousands of apartment rentals for visits of one or two weeks, or longer, in the international community that has developed around the southern beaches. Your travel agent or the nearest Spanish Tourist office can supply particulars on the apartment rentals, but keep your eye open for *se alquiler* (for rent) signs. Here are a few listings to get you started:

In the southern beach area:

Los Tilos, Avenida Espana 11, Playa del Inglés: 928-76 13 00.

Aguila Playa, Plaoleta Hibiscus 1, Playa del Inglés: 928-76 31 44.

Interclub Atlantico, Calle Los Jazmines 2, San Agustin: 928-76 07 70.

In Las Palmas:

Apartments are a bit more expensive here, but try Playa Sol, Paseo de Las Canteras 74: 928-26 14 80—it's very near the beach.

In the Country

There are inexpensive pensione-style accomodations in most small towns and villages. Gran Canarios have discovered the profits to be made in catering to the tourist dollar. These small hotels are usually quite acceptable, at sometimes one-tenth the price of the tourist hotels. You really get in touch with island life when you stay in one of these pensiones. The Tourist Office isn't much help here. Ask at the local bar or the market. Be sure to inspect the room before striking a deal; it is possible to bargain.

## *Camping*

There are several organized camping sites. One very pleasant, woodsy campground at Lomo de la Cruz, about fifteen miles from Las Palmas, has a bar and a swimming pool. There's a good beachside campsite at Guantanamo near Playa de Tauro that has restaurants, bars, showers and a children's playground.

Unlike on the other islands, you can run into problems trying to camp on the beach, especially in the south. Quite contrary to basic Spanish law, sections of the beach have been fenced off and "No Trespassing" signs have been put up. This isn't just a ploy to discourage itinerant international backpackers, because in some cases, the locals have been fenced out of their favorite fishing areas by English and German property owners. Spanish law is quite clear that beaches are common property for all to share, but once the fences were put up, it became necessary to take the international owners to court, where the case is slowly being heard.

There is no such problem in the mountains, where anyone with a sleeping bag is free to find a snug cave or camping area, atlhough it is polite to ask first.

# EATING AND DRINKING

## The Food

Not only are there outstanding Canarian seafood restaurants, but almost every type of international cuisine is available, including restaurants specializing in the various regional dishes of Mainland Spain. One of the best Galacian restaurants I've ever been to is in Las Palmas.

What is amazing is that even the restaurants that frankly cater to tourists by the busload are quite good. We once had lunch at a restaurant in the central mountains where we were seated just as a busload of English tourists came in; contrary to our fears, the lunch of Canarian fish soup and grilled rabbit was quite good. We lingered a bit, waiting for the bus trippers to leave. When the whole restaurant emptied, we took our coffee and dessert with a glass of the local sweet Malvasia to a window overlooking a spectacular canyon where we watched a couple of mid-sized hawks patrolling the terraced gardens below.

There is a wide choice of country restaurants that serve typical dishes of the island like roast leg of pork or a goat stew (rancho canario) with the local mojos.

Tapas are very popular in Las Palmas and are often on display at local bars, so if you know little Spanish, you can simply point to what you want. It's a tasty and inexpensive way to sample some of the local cuisine, with most dishes selling for $1 to $2.

You may want to finish your meal with one of the excellent cigars rolled on Gran Canaria, Tenerife and La Palma, such as the Puro de Marquez, made of pure Havana leaf and selling for just slightly over $1 each. In order to bring these back through US customs (Cuban cigars are banned), you can get a receipt for the cigars from the Canary Islands. Nowhere on the receipt or cigar package is it identified as Cuban tobacco.

## The Drink

Most of the local wines are dessert-style Malvasias. What little table wine is made on Gran Canaria seldom leaves the immediate area of the winery. But you needn't be fearful of running out of drink. The wines of the Peninsula are available everywhere and, in the international restaurants and hotels, you can order French and Italian vintages if you wish.

If you are on Gran Canaria only for sun and sand, the best plan is to stay in a hotel or apartment in the south, somewhere around Maspalomas, but if your goal is really to see the island, you should plan on spending at least a few days in Las Palmas. In fact, the city itself merits a close look, especially the old city or Vegueta, an area of small squares and narrow streets, buildings with carved Canarian balconies and a great deal of charm.

It was originally the home of the wealthier families, away from the noise and bustle of the port. It was built around a river gorge, the Barranco Guiniguada, which has been covered over and is now a road. There are several museums clustered in the area around the Cathedral of Santa Ana, so it is feasible to take a bus or taxi to the Plaza of Santa Ana in front of the cathedral and to base your explorations there.

The cathedral itself was founded in 1497, but wasn't actually finished until the nineteenth century. It's an odd but appealing blend of Gothic, neoclassical and Canarian architecture. There is a museum of religious art connected to the church, with a separate entry from Calle Espiritu Santo, a narrow passage connecting the plaza of Santa Ana with the Calle Colón. At number 1, there is a fifteenth century house made into a museum, displaying many artifacts from the period of conquest as well as documents and maps relating to Columbus and his voyages.

It's a very pleasant museum to wander about in. Canarian balconies overlook a central courtyard with a well, which Columbus is said to have used to supply his ships. It isn't known how long Columbus stayed on Gran Canaria or whether it was before or after his slightly scandalous sojourn on Gomera.

A few blocks up the hill from Santa Ana Plaza is the Museum of the Canaries on Calle Dr. Chil. It's an outstanding museum with an excellent collection of Guanche relics, including mummies, ceramics and jewelry. For a startling contrast, be sure to visit the Centro Atlantico de Arte Moderno, a few streets away on Calle Los Balcones. The museum is set in an eighteenth century building and retains its original facade; Francisco Sáinz de Oiza has designed the interior within a general framework of traditional Canarian design—but it is entirely modern! The four floors of exhibit space are arranged around a central, enclosed courtyard, echoing in form the colonial Canarian house.

Toward the ocean are the theater and opera house, built

GRAN CANARIA

GRAN CANARIA

GRAN CANARIA

Morro de La Vieja

LA ISLETA

Pta. de Bañaderos
Pta. de Arucas
Bañaderos
Cordones
Montaña de Arucas
Tenoya
Arucas
Tamaraceite
El Palmar
San Lorenzo
N.S. del Pino
La Calzada
Teror
MONTE COELLO
Tafira Baja
Tafira Alta
Santa Brígida
Mirador
Jinámar
La Atalaya
CALDERA BANDAMA
San Mateo
San Roque
Telde
Valsequillo
Caldera
O DE LAS NIVES

Las Canteras
PLAYA
PUERTO DE LA LUZ
PLAYA DE ALCARAVANERAS
LAS PALMAS
DE GRAN CANARIA

117

Playa La Laja

Peñascos

La Estrella
Playa S. Borondón
La Garita
PLAYA DE LA
Melenara       GARITA
PLAYA SALINETAS

Playa Tufia

Ruinas
Históricas

AEROPUERTO
DE GANDO
Barrio de
Triana      Pta. Gando

Sta. Lucía
Ingenio
Carrizal
Agüímes

aga

Lomo de
Los Letreros
Lago Edén

Playa de Las Cruces

Arinaga
Pta. del Mato

Sardina
Vecindario
Aldea Blanca
OYA DE TOLEDO
Cañón del Aguila
Juan Grande
La Caleta
Pta. Tenefe
El Matorral
Barco Quebrado
Pta. Gaviota

Pta. de Tarajalillo
PLAYA SAN AGUSTIN
Playa de Las Burras
AYA DEL INGLES
alomas
TA DE MASPALOMAS

in 1919 and decorated by Néstor Martin Fernandez de la Torre, a Canarian painter of some fame. He also designed a model Canary Island village, Pueblo Canario. This is nearby, part of the Parque Doramas, a welcome oasis of green within the sprawling capital. A museum in the park shows his work.

The Calle Mayor de Triana, filled with fine shops and upscale restaurants and bars, ends at San Telmo park and the tiny fifteenth century chapel of San Telmo. The park is near the site of the city's first pier, but is better known today for the old army headquarters, the building where General Franco was stationed when he set afoot the coup that led to the bitter Spanish Civil War of 1936-39.

The main beach of Las Palmas is the Las Canteras area, a gently curving two and one-half mile stretch of white sand along a wide promenade. Las Canteras is a favorite vacation spot for Mainland Spanish who come here in the summer to escape the Peninsula heat. This is truly an international zone, with Chinese restaurants, English pubs, German beer halls, pizza parlors and basic Spanish bars set down higgledy-

**THE COLUMBUS HOUSE IN LAS PALMAS, GRAN CANARIA**

piggledy all along the beach front.

It is more than slightly bizarre to see a salon offering expensive fur coats next door to an Indian bazaar selling cheap brass trinkets from Asia. One gets the full impact along Las Canteras that the Canary Islands' status as a free port actually means something. Scandinavians, Germans, Italians, French and Arabs come to Las Palmas to buy their furs duty-free, then stay to enjoy the sun and maybe to buy a carpet from Afghanistan before jetting back home.

It's a fascinating place simply to people-watch, on both the beach and the promenade. One can stake out a good spot on the beach by renting chairs and an umbrella (which will be welcome if you plan to spend much time in the Canarian sun) anywhere along the beach. You can rent sports equipment at several spots along the beach and minor board surfing is possible at times. The surf is not high here, but the wave action is surprisingly strong and even a small breaker can give you a decent ride. Windsurfing equipment is also available.

After a day of urban sightseeing, you deserve a good dinner. The choice is wide in Las Palmas, but one place that was especially memorable for us was Restaurante Marisqueria or Casa Julio. If you give either name to a taxi driver, you will arrive at the right place. Ask to be seated upstairs where the decor and the service are better.

The menu is quite large, but if you know enough Spanish, ask what the specials are or what is freshest. If you don't speak the language, get a glass of wine, relax for a while and observe the other tables to see what looks inviting. Then order, pointing when necessary. Don't let a waiter rush you. If Salma a la Plancha is available, it is a real treat. This flaky fish is sweet and moist and really too delicate for the mojo sauce that is served with it. Eat it straight. Also, parrillada, a mixed grill of whole small fish, breca, fillets, salmonette, mussels and langostinos, is a beautiful display and a delectable eating experience. Several mojo sauces are offered with the parrillada.

Outside of Las Palmas, head for the mountain—Mt. Tejeda to be exact. It's just about in the center of the island and in some of the most spectacular country around. There are several routes to Tejeda, since most island roads seem to lead there eventually. If you drive south out of Las Palmas, it could be the start of a one-day circle route. Turn inland at the thriving city of Telde, then follow the signs toward Valesquilla, which was a major Guanche village. Between Valesquilla and the tiny village of Tenteniguada, the road passes through rugged mountains and groves of lemons and almonds. There are a lot of caves in this area, many previously inhabited by Guanches.

More to the immediate point, there are several decent roadside restaurant/bars along this route to get a good cup of espresso if you left Las Palmas too early to indulge. Perhaps a café carajillo might be in order, to brace yourself for the day's driving. A carajillo is the same formula as the café correcto in Italian—coffee with brandy. In Peninsula Spain you can ask for anis instead of brandy, but that's unusual in the Canaries. Be prepared for an occasional giggle from a waitress when you order, because on the Mainland, carajillo is also the slang term for "small penis."

The village of Tenteniguada is worth a look in itself. It's built into a terraced hillside with apparently every scrap of dirt put to use. Beyond the village, the road begins to climb and you will notice some chilly winds blowing—I hope you remembered your sweater or even a light jacket, because those winds can turn downright cold by the time you get to Tejeda.

A few miles past Tenteniguada is the small town of San Mateo, which is an important cheese-making center, well-known on the island for a dry sheep cheese called queso negro. An excellent museum called Cho Zacarias is in a restored Canarian farmhouse. It even has a tiny working winery where you get a glass of local vino at the end of the tour.

After San Mateo, you will soon come to a junction in the

road; the right fork goes to Teror and the left to Cruz de Tejeda, a tiny village close to the Parque Nacional de Tejeda. Nearby is the Hosteria Cruz de Tejeda, a former Parador recently turned into a restaurant. The building is another Néstor de la Torre design. The food is typical Canarian fare and the view is splendid. Vendors sell handicrafts, local honey, cheese and produce all along the road near the village, which is set in a magnificent volcanic valley. Look for a snack of bienmesabe ('tastes good to me'), a local sweet made from almonds and honey.

Beyond Tejeda, take the road signed for Artenara. It's roughly an eight mile drive through a charming pine forest with cave houses where residents have built tasteful façades, many with wide view windows and beautifully carved wooden doors that open directly into the hillside. Outside, the ever-present television antennae stick right up out of the ground. There are caves on Gran Canaria that have probably been inhabited, off and on, for a couple thousand years, perhaps longer. Caves, after all, are a very practical habitat; they are cool in summer and warm in winter and pose very little danger of catching fire.

The Guanches understood this very well. Because they lacked the tools to build artificial caves, they had a limited number of sites to choose from. Faced with this primitive housing shortage, the Guanche aristocracy took the caves and left the commoners to construct stone and wood houses on the plains below.

Modern cave dwellers have used chain saws to work the soft volcanic stone, cutting furniture out of the walls of the cave itself, a tidy savings in home furnishing expense right there.

Yet even keeping in mind the practicality of cave life, it is a little strange to pull into the parking lot outside a cave bar. There are several of these in the north of Gran Canaria, especially in the area of the Barranco de Guayadeque.

And there are other caves-gone-commercial just beyond Tejeda in Artenara, a village above the cloud level. An excellent restaurant there called Meson la Silla serves local food. The restaurant closes at sunset and does not seem to have a telephone. There's sure to be someone sitting in the green and leafy central plaza by the church who can tell you how to find it. There are also signs for the restaurant.

The entrance leads you through a cave, but it unexpectedly opens out into a terrace with a fantastic view over a jumbled upland volcanic plain. One highlight of the view is the Roque Nublo and the Roque Bentaiga, sacred places for the Guanches. Artenara also has a cave church, which can be identified by its bell and by a rock arch topped with a squat rocky cross that sticks up out of the bare hillside.

Beyond Artenara, the roads are not very reliable, but hiking is excellent here and around the small village of Cueve Grande, south of Tejeda. During the spring, you can find several choice wildflowers in the area, including a pink-purple species of orchid and several yellow-flowered endemic shrubs in the Aeonium species.

After returning to Tejeda, head toward Valleseco and Teror. Regarded as the most typical Canarian town on the island, Teror has many lovely old houses with wooden balconies and beautifully carved doors. Teror is also the chief religious center on the island. The town is important because the Virgin appeared to the first bishop of Gran Canaria on December 8, 1482 in the branches of a pine tree.

The first chapel of the Nuestra Señora del Pino was built in 1515, replaced in 1692 by a larger church, and then destroyed by an explosion and fire in 1718. The tower survived and has been incorporated into the present church, built in the 1760s. A marvelous statue of the Virgin, about three feet tall, also survived the explosion and fire. The statue, said to date from the eighteenth century, is unusual in that the two sides of the Virgin's face are different; one side is sorrowful, the other joyful. The Virgin is surrounded by a splendid display of silver and has—as do most such statues in Spain— a magnificent wardrobe made over the centuries by the islanders.

Teror has a good museum, just opposite the church, with exhibits of life in the early days on Gran Canaria. There are also several good tapas bars. Look for the Bar Americano, opposite the church or the Bar Royale on Calle Gonzales X, which has several good tapas for under $1. The Royale also has interesting murals depicting Canarian life, painted in the style of the great Mexican muralist, Diego Rivera.

Before leaving Teror, it is important to think about lunch. There's the Balcón de Zamor near the village, with basic Canarian cuisine and a good view down a terraced canyon. Also, the hosteria Parador is only a few kilometers away. On the other hand, you could push on to the coast and have fresh seafood at several good restaurants, such as Restaurante Dedo de Dios on the beach at Puerto de las Nieves.

**· · · · · · · · · · · · · SNAPSHOT**

*We had just finished a long lunch of local seafood, lingering for a brandy and cigar at a restaurant with the unlikely name of Dedo de Dios, or Finger of God, in Puerto de las Nieves. From our window table, we had watched three fishermen bring a boat up onto the sand beach a few yards from our table and overturn it on the sand to scrape the bottom.*

*We had spent some time studying the rocky cliffs down the coast, looking for the solitary rock that stuck up into the air like "the finger of God." We saw several candidates, but I'm not sure that any of them were actually God's finger. However, our mission to Puerto de las Nieves, a pleasant little fishing village on the northwest coast about a sixty-minute drive from Las Palmas, had to do with the Virgén de las Nieves, not God's finger.*

*The Ermita de las Nieves is a sixteenth century church dedicated to the Virgin of the snows. It contains the central section of a particularly fine fifteenth century Flemish triptych (the other two parts are in the parish church at Agaete—*

123

all three parts are displayed together once a year during an August festival) and a Mudéjar carved ceiling above the altar. The Virgin, attributed to the Dutchman Joos Van Cleve, is absolutely remarkable. The Madonna looks eager and full of life, her eyes smiling out of the painting, while the Christ child has a bright, laughing face. How such a work ever ended up there in a church built by poor fishermen is a great puzzle, for it is a stunning work.

However, the small church is now kept locked and it is necessary to hunt down the caretaker, Antonio, to open it for viewing. We had left word at Antonio's house before lunch to meet us at the church at 4 p.m., which seemed to be ample time for all of us to finish our meals. We walked back to the church (you can go right through the whole town in ten minutes), but Antonio wasn't there. We went back to Antonio's house. No Antonio.

Not back from lunch yet. Check at the Dedo de Dios.

Perhaps Antonio had lunched there as well?

No, he would be in the bar.

Yes, the barman had seen Antonio, but not for a good hour.

Did he know where to find him?

Why did we wish to see Antonio?

The church, we explained. We wanted to see the interior of the church.

Ah! In that case, I think I can find him for you. Come with me.

We walked back through town (many of the faces on the street were beginning to look familiar) to a small house set back in a garden behind a fisherman's bar on the harbor.

Wait here. Antonio may be taking a nap, he said, and smiled and winked.

We waited, watching our volunteer guide as he pounded on the door of the house, shouting something we couldn't follow. At length, a young woman stuck her head out the window and exchanged a few words with our guide. In a couple of minutes Antonio, a tall, bald man with a *weatherbeaten face who looked to be in his mid-fifties (we learned later that he was seventy-eight) appeared, grinning.*

*We apologized for interrupting his 'siesta.*

*No, we were assured. It was no problem. He could always return later.*

*After the tour of the church, Antonio mentioned that it is best to ask for him and his key at the Dedo de Dios bar. They always know where to find him, while his daughter at home might not know just exactly where he would be.*

Either before or after lunch, backtrack a few kilometers from Teror to the main road and follow the signs to Firgas and Banadero, where you will be back on the coast. It's a nice drive along the north coast of the island, with several likely surfing beaches and good picnic spots between Banadero and the village of San Felipe, where the road turns inland for Agaete and Puerto de las Nieves.

Near Puerto de las Nieves is the village of Agaete, an agricultural center, known in other parts of the island as the center of the festival of Bajada de la Rama, held during the first week of August. The festival of Rama goes back to Guanche times, when the aborigines would march down the barranco to the sea (the present site of Puerto de las Nieves). They carried palm branches with which they would beat the surf in an effort to raise some rain showers. The modern-day festival follows pretty much along the same lines, except that the modern marchers direct their prayers for rain to the Virgin of the Snows (Señora de las Nieves).

The barranco de Agaete is a four-and-a-half-mile long green and well-watered canyon that extends up the mountain from Agaete to Los Berrazales. In this tiny settlement, there is a hotel and restaurant named the Princesa Guayarmina after the last Guanche princess. The drive up the barranco can be a little hair-raising (especially when you meet a tourist bus on a curve), but on the whole the road is good and the drive is certainly worth it.

Beyond Nieves, the highway stays close to the coast,

with several good swimming and diving beaches, especially around Puerto de la Aldea, where the road turns inland to San Nicolas de Tolentino. A secondary road opened recently over the mountains to the pretty village of Mogan, from which a main road leads down to the tourist centers of the south coast. Follow this route if you want to do a circuit of the island, but if so, you should book a room in Mogan or on the coast below Mogan. You can make it around the island in one day, but what's the rush?

Our personal choice was to turn back after lunch at Puerto de las Nieves, following the fast coast route back to Las Palmas. We wanted a quick swim on Las Canteras beach before a few tapas, as we were not really hungry enough for a proper meal. We walked up the beach a couple of blocks to Casa Gallega, where we sat at the bar and ordered several little dishes of Gallegan specialties. We washed them down with the eminently drinkable Gallegan wines, which come in little bowls that look like sushi dipping bowls. It's very easy to drink a lot of wine in these tiny bowls without being aware you're doing so.

We had a perfect meal that night: a bowl of miniature clams in a white wine and garlic sauce, a slice of empanada and the famous Gallegan double-crusted pie filled with tomatoes, onions, salt cod and something else that I don't quite remember—could that be the result of all that light and delicious wine? The food and service were excellent and I would have liked to return the next night for dinner but, alas, that will have to wait until the next trip.

## . . . . . . . . . . . . . . SNAPSHOT

*The beaches of the southern tourist areas are utterly spectacular, and no matter how crowded the various resorts may seem, it is always possible to find a near-empty stretch of beach to call your very own. There are also several marinas where boats can be chartered for fishing or diving.*

*It is also important to keep in mind that the tourist crush on Gran Canaria is actually much less than in Honolulu or on the Florida Gold Coast.*

*And if the beach life becomes too bland, it's easy and cheap to rent a car for the day and escape to the interior for the breathtaking mountain scenery Gran Canaria has to offer. Or you can go to the relatively undeveloped western and northern coast for a quiet lunch in a fishing village right out of the nineteenth century.*

*Something you won't find in Hawaii or Florida.*

## Useful Information

Tourist Office, Plaza Ramón Franco, Santa Catalina Park, Las Palmas: 928-26 46 23.

Museums

Canarian Museum, Calle Doctor Chil 25, Las Palmas: 928-31 56 00. Well-displayed exhibits on the Guanches and their culture. Closed on public holidays.

Casa de Colon, Calle Colón 1, Las Palmas: 928-31 12 55. Good exhibits relating to Columbus and early life on the island in a restored eighteenth century Canarian home. Closed Sundays and public holidays.

Centro Atlantico de Arte Moderno, Calle Los Balcones 9 and 11, Las Palmas: 928-31 18 24. Closed Sundays and public holidays.

Marinas for renting water sports equipment, chartering sailboats, fishing boats, etc.

Puerto Rico Marina, Puerto Rico: 928-74 57 57.

Escuela Territorial de Vela de Puerto Rico, Puerto Rico: 928-74 53 31.

Real Club Náutico de Gran Canaria, Puerto de la Luz: 928-24 52 02.

Puerto Deportivo de las Palmas, Avenida Maritima: 928-74 57 57.

Pasito Blanco Yacht Club, Playa Morgán: 928-76 22 59.

Sporting Center of the Hotel Don Gregory, San Augustin

gives instruction in windsurfing and diving and rents equipment: 928-76 26 62.

Sun Club, Playa del Inglés: 928-76 31 32.

Other

Aeroclub Maspalomas: 928-76 24 47.

Picadero Oasis Maspalomas: 928-76 23 78 for riding and horse rental.

Campo de Golf de Maspalomas: 928-76 25 81. An 18-hole golf course, open to the public.

**THE PLEASURES OF LA PALMA INCLUDE MODERN
RESORTS AND RUSTIC COASTLINES**

**THE TRADITIONAL TIMPLE IS HAND CRAFTED
IN THE OLD TRADITION**

**JUAN PARRILLA MEDINA,
PLAYING THE TIMPLE,
A TRADITIONAL MUSICAL
INSTRUMENT OF LANZAROTE.**

VINEYARDS, STRUGGLING FOR SURVIVAL IN THE HARSH VOLCANIC SOIL OF LANZAROTE. THESE VINES ARE WELL AND TRULY STRESSED.

CÉSAR MANRIQUE'S FAMED DRAGON SCULPTURE AT
THE MIRADOR DE LA PEÑA ON EL HIERRO.

CÉSAR MANRIQUE'S LATEST CREATION, THE JARDIN
DE CACTUS ON HIS NATIVE ISLAND OF LANZAROTE.

GOATS AND SHEEP SHARE THE PASTURE ON THE
ROCKY ISLAND OF FUERTEVENTURA.

THE HOTEL PUNTEGRANDE, THE WORLD'S SMALLEST HOTEL, ON HIERRO.

THE INTERIOR OF THE MIRADOR DE LA PEÑA, DESIGNED BY CÉSAR MANRIQUE, ON THE ISLAND OF HIERRO.

LOOKING DOWN ON THE TRANQUIL WESTERN SHORE OF HIERRO.

LOOKING OUT OVER THE ATLANTIC ON THE WEST COAST OF HIERRO FROM A WINDOW OF THE RESTAURANT NOEMI OVERLOOKING THE HOTEL PUNTAGRANDE, THE WORLD'S SMALLEST HOTEL.

**THE MARKETPLACE IN SANTA CRUZ DE TENERIFE, THE ISLAND'S CAPITAL.**

**A DRAGON TREE IN LA OROTAVA.**

**VISITORS TO THE CANARIES CAN EAT VERY WELL FROM THE BOUNTY OF THE ISLANDS.**

# LA PALMA

The island of San Miguel de La Palma lies in the northwestern corner of the Canarian archipelago. At 282 square miles, it is the fifth largest of the Canary Islands. The island stretches about twenty-nine miles from north to south and about seventeen miles from east to west. With about 80,000 residents, it is the third most populated of the islands. About 20,000 people live in the capital city of Santa Cruz.

A rugged mountain chain towers over the northern and central parts of the island. The highest peak is Roque de los Muchachos, reaching 7874 feet at the edge of a huge volcanic crater that dominates the northern half of the island. In relation to its size, La Palma (as it is known to its friends) has the highest altitude in the world.

Like Hierro and Gomera, La Palma welcomes tourists, who can arrive either by jet or ferry, but is far from presenting itself as a standard tourist treadmill. The chief occupation of the island inhabitants is still agriculture, with the next highest number involved in small, low-tech manufacturing such as making cigarettes and cigars.

La Palma has one resource that is denied to most of the rest of the Canaries—water—which supports a major agriculture export industry based on bananas. La Palma produces almost one-third of the total bananas on the Canary Islands.

Like all the islands, La Palma was raided for slaves during the thirteenth and fourteenth centuries. The Spanish attempted to conquer it as early as 1447, but did not succeed until 1492, when the Castilian Alonso Fernández de Lugo gained control of the island through a combination of arms and trickery. One of the island's folk heroes is Tanausú, a king of the aboriginal Guanches (who called themselves Benaohare on La Palma). Tanausú held out against the Castilian troops from deep within his mountain stronghold. He was tricked into coming out to meet the Spanish and was promptly seized. The story goes that Tanausú starved himself to death on the ship that took him to Spain, away from his beloved island.

La Palma was the object of frequent pirate raids in the sixteenth and seventeenth centuries. Sir Francis Drake even attempted to seize the capital, but was beaten off. As might be expected, the pirates and raiders were attracted by the wealth of Santa Cruz, one of the busiest and richest ports in all of Spain, based on exports of sugar cane and hardwood from the island's interior.

As on all the islands, the prevailing weather on La Palma is temperate, with very little temperature fluctuation, except in the mountains, where it can get chilly enough for heavy sweaters or jackets. The average annual temperature is in the 60s.

## WHERE TO STAY

*L*ike the other small and relatively untouristed islands of the Western Canaries, there are very few international hotels on La Palma, but there are a number of very good one- and two-star establishments, apartments, rooms and small pensiones. Only during the peak of the tourist season in July or August would there be any concern about finding accomodation on the spot, especially in Santa Cruz or in the second largest city, Los Llanos.

### Camping

There is one campground in the Parque Nacional

Caldera de Taburiente. Many informal campgrounds are scattered throughout the island. Inquire locally.

## WHAT TO DO

*L*a Palma has some of the best hiking in the Canaries. It is a botanical paradise with wildflowers year round and dozens of endemic trees and shrubs. The beaches are good for swimming, and the windsurfing and board surfing are good. There is excellent fishing and diving from chartered boats in Santa Cruz or other North Coast ports.

## WHAT TO EAT AND DRINK

### The Food

Here, as everywhere on the islands, the seafood steals the show, but there is also an abundance of local vegetables and fruits, including a great variety of tropical fruits— avocados, pineapples, oranges, papayas, pomegranates and, of course, bananas. The mix of tropical and temperate zone fruits in the same orchard is reminiscent of coastal California. One can see orange trees growing next to pear trees, with the brilliant blossoms of a plum tree next to an avocado with an almond tree close by.

There are good local cheeses, both fresh and smoked, mostly from goat milk. The parillada or mixed grill is very popular on La Palma, especially in the countryside, where you can order a huge plate of grilled lamb, sausage, rabbit, goat and chicken in whatever combination you might like. With a salad and roasted potatoes on the side, a pot of mojo sauce, a pitcher of local wine or a good bottled wine from the Mainland, this feast costs only a few dollars and will keep you happy for hours.

# Restaurants

La Palma probably has more than its fair share of good restaurants per square kilometer. If you are looking for haute cuisine, pack your bags and move on. On the other hand, if you are looking for honest, healthful food, skillfully and tastefully prepared, you're on the right island. From the dozens of fish restaurants along the rocky coast, to the country-style grill restaurants inland, La Palma is a trencherman's delight. There isn't a piece of plastic food on the island. Fast food is confined to a plate of olives in a local tapas bar.

Here are a few places we found particularly outstanding:

Bodegon Tamanca on the coast beyond El Paso, near the southern tip of the island: 922-46 07 06. The restaurant has been tunneled out of the hillside, as have an extensive series of wine caves where local wines are bought in and stored in huge old wooden vats. The restaurant is a great example of the parilla mixta, a style of cooking brought back from South America by Canarios who returned after finding their fortunes there. Or at least enough of a fortune to open a restaurant.

Bar Restaurante Las Brisas in Hoyo de Mazo: 922-44 01 79. A few miles from Santa Cruz, this restaurant has a full dinner menu, but also offers some very special tapas, such as rabbit in mojo sauce.

Meson del Mar in Puerto Espindola, a fishing village north of Santa Cruz. There is no telephone number. This seafood restaurant is right across from a small wharf. You can sit and watch the fishermen pull their catch from the water, while enjoying a grilled fish that, itself, must have come from the sea only a few hours before. Try to get a table on the narrow upstairs Canarian balcony—it's only one table wide—with its magnificent views of the coast.

Restaurant Bar Los Volcanes, Carretera General 72, Fuencaliente: 922-44 41 64. A delightful highway stop with good local sausages and grilled sweet sausages as tapas, and local sweet wine from a barrel (which is served with tasty almond cookies). Los Volcanes also has a few studio apartments looking out over the fields toward the sea. The rooms have balconies, private baths and three meals a day for 1500 pesetas each. When we were last there, that would be about $15 each!

## *The Wines*

There are excellent local wines on La Palma. Certainly worth a taste are the wines from Bodegas Teneguia and the co-op wines from Llanovid, both in Fuencaliente. The tradition of sweet wines is dying out on La Palma, as the commercial wineries believe the modern taste is entirely for dry wine. Nevertheless, it is still possible to find well made and sweetly delicious malvasias in local bars. These are invariably poured from an unlabeled bottle or directly from a small barrel behind the bar, which is filled at the bodega (most likely in someone's private cellar). Rum is also made on La Palma, as is a very sweet banana liqueur.

Modern viticulture does not exist on La Palma. One of the major vineyard areas was wiped out by a volcano in 1971, the last eruption on the islands. Nowhere did we see any trellised vines or any indication of special care in the vineyard beyond the ancient vasco , or head-pruned vines. These are trained close to the ground, with the bearing canes propped up on basketball-sized boulders to keep the grapes off the earth. The major grape grown now is the Palomino, used in the light white table wines of the island.

Flying into La Palma, the Iberia jet from Tenerife skims low across the shallow bay of Brena Baja. If the day is calm, the bay is flecked with small fishing boats and a few pleasure craft. The sea is an intense blue, too blue to be true, like a gaudy set from a 1950's Hollywood technicolor musical. The illusion is maintained when you look up and see the green mountain forests of La Palma beyond the bay.

La Palma lies directly in the path of the moisture-bearing northeast trade winds which bring more rain to the island than to any of the other Canaries. (They are the same trades that made Santa Cruz de la Palma such an attractive port in the days of sailing ships. You can simply coast in from the mainland.) The rain keeps La Palma green and has earned it the name La Isla Verde, the green island.

Most of the rain falls in the north, as the clouds from the Atlantic bump up against the central mountain range. An elaborate system of irrigation pipes carries the runoff water from the north all over the southern part of the island, bringing water to the banana plantations that march right down to the sea, as well as to vegetable gardens, vines and orchards that move in giant terraced steps up the hillsides.

La Palma is the only island in the Canaries with year-round running streams. Hiking one of the many trails into the Caldera de Taburiente, a national park, you are never far from the sound of running water, either from one of the many springs that burst from the canyon walls, or the Rio de las Angustias, which flows through the rift valley at the bottom of the Caldera.

The Caldera de Taburiente is a spectacular piece of country. It is the crater of an extinct volcano which collapsed about 400,000 years ago. The crater is 5.5 miles across with a sheer inner wall about 2300 feet high—almost half a mile. When the volcano collapsed, a valley opened up to the southwest, where the river now flows.

Three roads lead to the park. The easiest drive is from the town of El Paso, which leads to an overlook called Mirador La Cumbrecita. A trail starts there, as does an unpaved road that goes to another overlook.

A second road leads to the Rocque los Muchachos, the highest point on the island. You can reach that road from Briestas in the north or from Santa Cruz, after a very twisting drive through the mountains.

There is an unpaved road that starts in Los Llanos and descends to the river on the floor of the valley. Unless there

## LA PALMA

have been heavy rains, you can drive across the river to a lookout in the center of the valley. There are a number of tobacco farms in this area, though not as many as there once were, as the Canarian cigar industry has never achieved the international status that had been hoped for. The road continues past a number of waterfalls to a lookout spot in the center of the crater.

But the best way to look at the Caldera is on foot, hiking one of the trails that descend into the crater. You can obtain trail maps at the tourist office in Santa Cruz and, if you don't wish to rent a car, you can also arrange transportation there via tourist bus or taxi.

As you descend into the crater, you hike through Canarian pine, which line the walls; near the bottom, deciduous woods dominate and the forest floor is dotted with wildflowers.

With over 700 species of plants, La Palma is a virtual paradise for the botanist, whether professional or amateur. Not only are there tremendous numbers of wildflowers on the Isla Verde, but there are 70 endemic varieties of palm trees alone. Other endemic species include the Echium pininana, a spectacular plant with pale blue flowering spikes shooting ten to thirteen feet into the air.

An unusual park at Los Sauces, the Bosque Los Tilos, is an unlogged virgin forest of giant laurel, which contains plants found nowhere else in the world. As with the similar park on the island of Hierro, the United Nation operates this park as a unique biosphere. There are several hiking trails through the forest, with a trailhead at the park headquarters. You'll find the headquarters at the end of a gravel road that winds up from the coastal highway, north of Santa Cruz. An hour's stroll through this primitive, moss-green landscape is marvelously healing to the hurried modern soul.

Palmeros take the beauty of their island very seriously. They have managed to avoid some of the uglier excesses of tourism. Although they welcome tourists, they understand that the unspoiled beauty of the island is the greatest attraction they have to offer. For example, no billboards are permitted on La Palma (except at the airport) and there are regulations controlling artificial lighting at night. The

Palmeros' concern about lighting is twofold: first, they recognize it as a form of visual pollution but more importantly, they now understand the value of darkness in a purely scientific sense. Because its air is so pure, La Palma was chosen as the site for an observatory that houses the William Herschel Telescope, the largest in Europe and the third largest in the world. There is a sister observatory on Tenerife. Both are operated by the Instituto de Astrofisica de Canarias, based in Tenerife.

It doesn't take a giant telescope to demonstrate the clarity of the air in the Canaries. With a pair of ordinary binoculars, it is possible to see the headlights of individual cars driving in the Las Cañadas park on Tenerife's Mt. Teide, over eighty miles from La Palma. Also from La Palma, you can spot the lights of planes as they approach the airport on the island of Madeira, some 250 miles to the north.

. . . . . . . . . . . . . **SNAPSHOT**

*The studio was difficult enough to find in the daylight, I'm sure. And despite careful instructions, we seemed to be lost—and late. It was long past sunset, that deep twilight time when the eyes don't seem to focus exactly as they should. We were on an unpaved track, looking for the studio of two local potters who sign themselves Ramón y Vina. They also operate a souvenir shop called El Molino on the highway near Hoyo de Mazo, but we had made an appointment to see them in their studio, to see them in action.*

*Ramón and Vina specialize in exact reproductions of Guanche pottery, duplicating the ancient shapes and proportions of the few pieces of Guanche pottery that have been found intact. They use no wheels in making the pottery—only the ancient hand-shaped method and precise measuring tools so that the reproduction is the same to the last centimeter.*

*The track became so rough, or at least seemed so in the*

*dim twilight, that we finally parked the car in a turnout and continued on foot. We shouted from time to time, hoping to raise a reply from the studio, which we knew had to be somewhere on the dark hillside above us. There were a few twinkling lights ahead, but surely they were all too far away to be our destination.*

*At last, our shouts were answered and Ramon came down a path from the side, seeming to come straight out of a bush. Flashing what turned out to be a very efficient three-battery torch, he led us up a steep, rocky path to the studio, perched on the hillside like the nest of a hawk.*

*Inside, a small fire burned on the grate against the cool night breeze. Vina had given up on us and had gone into town for groceries, but Ramón was glad to show us his technique, his modern homage to a Guanche theme. The pot seemed to leap to life under his hands, which worked constantly, shaping, directing the flow of the clay.*

*We watched, almost without speaking, remembering that the pattern he was shaping was thousands of years old, a pattern that had been followed by Guanche men and women long before Spain was even a united country. While the Moors were still the lords of La Mancha and Castile, Guanche hands had been shaping a pot such as the one we saw building before us.*

*Later, we stepped out of the tiny studio into full darkness. The sky was brilliant with stars, as it usually is on La Palma. The same stars that were brightening the skies of La Palma centuries before, perhaps when the original Guanche pot we had just seen reproduced was first made.*

Stargazing is one of the major nighttime attractions on La Palma. Even in the capital of Santa Cruz, the discos are thin on the ground. But during the day, Santa Cruz shines. There is an expansive malecon, or seawall, at the harbor, with the broad Avenida Maritima bordering the water. There are a number of restaurants and hotels along the Maritima, but the most attractive part of the city is uphill from the harbor. Walk up the Avenida El Puente a few blocks to the Calle O'Daly—named after an Irish merchant—and the Plaza de España, a triangular plaza. Across the way is the *ayuntamiento*, or town hall. Look at the carved wooden ceiling above the stairs that lead from the ground floor to the first floor.

Next to the Plaza España is the Church of El Salvador, with a portal dating from 1503 and a beautifully carved Mudejar ceiling, based on designs from Portugal.

On the plaza, you can also see several eighteenth century historic homes with beautiful Canarian wood balconies. The parador in Santa Cruz has copied this style of architecture.

There are number of small squares—many with fountains—in Santa Cruz, which invite the walker to linger for a cup of espresso or a glass of wine. Sometimes the architectural displays of the more ordinary houses on these little squares are more fascinating than the grander efforts of the historic homes and churches. One can see up close the intricate carved wood on a railing or the happy contrast of a pot of red geraniums against a blue painted balcony.

The Calle Perez de Brito is a particularly good street for plaza hopping, as it winds up the hillside toward the Barranco de las Nieves (usually dry), where there is an ambitious maritime museum, the Barco de la Virgen. The concrete museum is an exact replica, in fact, of Columbus' ship, the Santa Maria. Palmeros believe Columbus stopped at Santa Cruz on one of his trips to the New World. There is no evidence that he did. On the other hand, there is no evidence that he didn't. And it makes a good excuse for a museum.

Day tripping out of Santa Cruz can be easily divided into two to four routes. The most basic is a southern and a northern day. Either or both of these days can be very happily extended, so try to keep a flexible schedule. La Palma has a way of grabbing the unwary. There is also a central route, if you have the time, which steals pieces from the northern and southern route. Finally, it is quite feasible to make a day's excursion to the Rocque de los Muchachos.

In general, the northern route hugs the cliff in scary blind curves above deep cut barrancas. It is necessary to make frequent stops, not just to take a deep breath before plunging onto the next few kilometers of curves, but also to have a close look at this incredibly beautiful coastline. The only other coast that comes to mind as being even a close match is the rugged Big Sur coast of Central California. Frightening as the curves may be, the highway is very well engineered, traffic is light and, after a few kilometers, it becomes clear that one is probably safer here than on many European or American autoways.

Only nine kilometers north of Santa Cruz is the small town of Puntallana with the sixteenth century church of San Juan, which has a very good Flemish carving of the same century. There is a wealth of Flemish art on La Palma, reflecting the riches of the island's past, when art from the northernmost reaches of the Spanish empire could be bought with gold won from the sugar cane and lumber trade.

Twenty-eight kilometers from Santa Cruz is San Andrés y Sauces, the chief agricultural town of the northern part of the island. There is a lovely central plaza in San Andrés, with flower beds laid out to spell the name of the town. The road to Bosque Los Tilos begins at San Andrés.

If you left Santa Cruz in the morning and had a leisurely drive up the coast, you would reach Puerto Espindola by noon. Drive into the southern end of the town, turning off the main highway onto a narrow lane with banana groves on the right, and white, balconied houses on the left. When you reach the waterfront, turn left. In a few hundred yards, there is an incredible natural rock swimming pool, known locally as El Charco Azul. It's a splendid place for a before-lunch swim if the day is warm. All around you, the waves crash against the rocks as if determined to tear La Palma loose from its moorings. The pool, which the waves and tidal action have carved out over the centuries, remains calm, although the water is constantly refreshed as waves break over the surrounding rocks. The water is a glass-clear, intense blue, so it's possible even for a casual swimmer to spot tiny crabs and other marine life.

After your dip, follow the road a few hundred yards further to a two-story restaurant called El Meson Mar, just across the street from a favorite local fishing spot. We arrived a little early, so we went into the downstairs bar and ordered two glasses of rum, one white and one dark, which were produced a few doors down the street. With the rum we got a plate of hot pulpo (octopus). We took a table on the lower balcony to watch the fishermen in action until our table in the upstairs restaurant was ready.

Rum is often taken with a late breakfast snack on the Canaries, as it is cheaper than the brandy or añis that would typically be drunk with coffee (sometimes in the coffee) on the Mainland. The white rum had an herbal, vegetal taste, but the caramel in the dark rum masked this flavor, making the dark slightly preferable.

The pulpo were delicious; they had been stewed with green peppers and olive oil, a simple dish which hit the spot after a morning of sightseeing.

Upstairs, the restaurant filled quickly—mostly with locals—but we had secured a table earlier on the narrow balcony outside. We were so close to the sea, it seemed, that the fish we ordered for lunch could have jumped out of the surf into the pan.

We began lunch with Sopa de Pescado, an intensely flavored fish broth with rice and bits of fish that benefited from an added spoonful of mojo verde. The sauce was a sharp flavored combination of green pepper, garlic, parsley, olive oil and vinegar. I used to think that only Mediterranean chefs produced perfectly fried fish, but the Canarians have this talent too. The small, fried Cabrillo served next was crispy on the outside and moist and tender on the inside, with not a speck of grease.

The road pushes on beyond Espindola, turning away from the coast into the northern part of the island. From there, the road goes to Santo Domingo de Garafia, where it turns back south.  Not long ago, this was one of the wildest areas anywhere in Spain, with communication to the outside world limited to mule trails and small coasting ships that find scant anchorage on the rugged north coast.  It's a dramatic, beautiful coast, though largely inaccessible to ordinary cars. There are a handful of roads—some paved, some unpaved— that twist down to tiny coastal villages like Gallegos and Franceses, where people probably don't see a tourist from one month to the next.

You can follow the road around the island, back through Los Llanos and El Paso into Santa Cruz, but that makes for a very long day trip and would leave little time to really appreciate being there.  The best plan is to turn back at Garafia and retrace your route to Santa Cruz (there are always things to see that you missed the first time), getting back in time for a good dinner and bottle of wine.  Maybe you would prefer a lighter evening of tapas in Santa Cruz or on the road between Breña Alta and Mazo, south of Santa Cruz.  Here, you'll find a number of good bar-restaurants and parrilladas where one can order a small mixed grill.

The main southern route includes the central area of the island and the village of Las Nieves with the Church of Nuestra Señora de las Nieves, Our Lady of the Snows.  The present church dates from the seventeenth century, although there was certainly a church on the spot much earlier.  From the outside, the church is quite lovely.  It is set in a small square with a cobblestone pavement amid jacaranda trees. There is an outdoor restaurant behind the church with a view back toward Santa Cruz and the sea.

The wooden ceiling is decorated in the Portuguese style and the church contains a number of sixteenth century Flemish statues, again, typical of religious art in the Canaries from that period.

But the focus of the church (and of the religious life of La Palma) is the small clay Gothic statue of the Virgin, who has been worshipped since the fifteenth century.  The Virgin is situated high above an incredibly carved Baroque silver altar and is beautifully dressed in robes decorated with pearls, rubies and other precious stones.

The small figure, credited with many local miracles, spends most of her time above the altar, but comes out every year in August for a parade around the church. Every five years, last in 1990, the Descent of the Virgin, La Palma's grandest fiesta, takes place. The small figure is then taken on a walk to the cathederal in Santa Cruz, along with many pieces of her altar, which the pilgrims carry ahead of her.

The celebration goes on for weeks and features dancing, parades, arts and crafts fairs and a general good time for all. Men and women both wear traditional costumes whose dominant colors are black, cream and red. This fiesta·has become so important that La Palma residents who have immigrated to Central and South America often return for the Descent.

Just beyond the church is a good local restaurant, the Chipi-Chipi, famous for its grills. Nearby is a handicraft shop and, just beyond that, the Mirador de la Concepcion, with a widescreen view of Santa Cruz and its harbor.

Past the Mirador is a tunnel through the wall of an old volcanic crater, and just two and a half miles beyond the tunnel is an unpaved road to the right. Unless it is raining, most cars can drive on it. Follow the signs toward La Caldera and El Paso. You will pass through Breña Alta, about eight or nine kilomters from Santa Cruz. It's rich farming land with palm trees and the legendary Canarian Dragon Tree (see description in Tenerife section). Breña Alta is the chief cigar making area of·La Palma. There are also handmade hats, baskets and other goods made of palm leaves and straw.

El Paso has a flourishing silk industry as well. Several workshops in the town welcome visitors. Beyond El Paso is Llanos de Aridane, the second largest city on the island, with about 15,000 inhabitants. Llanos is set in a sea of banana and avocado trees. It's a pleasant place to stop for a snack before pushing on to the coast and area around Teneguia, where the island's last volcanic eruption took place on October 26, 1971.

You can drive right out onto the lava field on marked roads, but don't stray from those areas. The volcanic ash is deep and it's quite easy for a car to get bogged down. The pathway around the central crater, the Volcan de San Antonio, offers wonderful views of the coast and the Atlantic. Standing in the wind sweeping off the sea, it's easy to believe that nothing stands between you and the Antarctic but several thousand miles of chilly winds.

The eruption covered a flourishing vineyard area and the local farmers are slowly reclaiming it, digging down through the lava to replant vines in the soil, then building low rock walls around the small vineyard areas to help protect them from the winds.

We stopped the car to look at the wind-twisted vines—the walls certainly didn't block the gusts at all—and noticed that the tips of the branches were beginning to swell; it was almost budbreak. There they were, those slender, fragile looking vines, pushing roots deep into the volcanic earth to bring us the gift of wine.

It was a reassuring sight.

. . . . . . . . . . . . . **SNAPSHOT**

*I had lingered perhaps a bit too long over a last glass of sweet wine and an aromatic black cigar at the Bar Los Volcanes in Fuencaliente. The barman served the wine with little spicy sausages and it was truly hard to stop eating and drinking. He took me to see a vacant studio apartment upstairs with a sweeping view down toward the Atlantic. I looked around the sparsely furnished but comfortable room and imagined waking up each morning to the distant sound of the surf, the morning sunlight edging through the glass door that led onto the balcony.*

*Yes, my Mac could go just there on the writing desk, with a few books on the TV stand. (I would ask him to move the TV out.) And, at the rent he was asking, I could easily stay for*

*months and months, writing that great American novel,
hiking on the hillsides, identifying the hundreds of wildflowers on La Palma.*

*The lines of Elinor Wylie's poem "Wild Peaches" came to
me:*

*"Peaches grow wild, and pigs can live in clover;*
*A barrel of salted herrings lasts a year;*
*The spring begins before the winter's over."*

*From the window at the back, I could see fig trees and
vines sprawling up the hillside. A yellow cat, lazing on a rock
wall that enclosed a kitchen garden, yawned in the last rays
of the setting sun and looked up at me as if to say, "Why, yes.
It's all possible. This is La Palma, after all. You needn't hurry
away."*

## Useful Information

The Tourist Office is at Calle O'Daly 8, Santa Cruz:
922-41 21 06.

LA PALMA

146

# TENERIFE

With 792 square miles and about 650,000 inhabitants, Tenerife is the largest of the Canary Islands, both in size and in population. At 12,198 feet, Mount Teide, the snow-covered peak that dominates the island's landscape, is the highest mountain, not only in the Canaries, but in all of Spain. The name Tenerife is of Guanche origin, meaning snow-covered mountain. (Most place names in the island chain beginning with "T" are derived from Guanche words.)

Tenerife was the last island to fall to the Spanish conquerors, though not from want of trying. There were many attempts all through the fifteenth century, but the Guanches—divided into nine kingdoms or menceys—put up a strong resistance. Finally, in 1494, the Spanish made various promises and won four of the kingdoms, giving them a base from which to fight the remaining kingdoms. The key battle took place on Christmas day, 1495. When the last Guanche king, Bentor, saw that his people had lost the fight, he hurled himself over a cliff in an act of ritual suicide. Some few warriors took to the mountains and put up a token resistance for several months, but the conquest was complete before the end of 1496.

Teide (pronounced tay day) is still an active volcano, as a brisk hike to the summit demonstrates. Many smoke holes—some quite large—belch sulphurous fumes. Most of the island is subject to volcanic activity. The last eruption was in 1909, though, except for the center of the old crater, Las Cañadas del Teide, most of the lava flows are now overgrown.

Tenerife has much more moisture than the other islands and is green most of the year, except for a small area in the south, which is semi-desert because the rain clouds are blocked by the central mountain range. The moisture on the island comes both from normal rainfall and from "horizontal rain," a phenomenon found also on the neighboring island of La Palma. This horizontal rain happens when trade-blown rain clouds come in off the Atlantic and stall over the island at higher elevations.

The island also has horizontal wells, as do La Palma, Gomera and Hierro. Instead of drilling vertical shafts to reach water, pipes are driven into the hillsides, tapping the underground water supply. Much of Tenerife's water comes from condensation, as trees draw water from the clouds and fog and filter it into underground streams.

The north coast of Tenerife—which catches the brunt of the trade winds—is often foggy and cloudy, with rugged cliffs rising sharply from the sea amid a scattering of black-sand beaches. It's a rich agricultural area and the main vine-growing region of the island. The southern shore is flatter, with a wide plain sloping gently to the sea and some fine sandy beaches. The main beach resort areas are on the southwest shore, roughly between Punta de la Rasca and as far north as Los Gigantes, where the central mountain range abruptly meets the sea in a massive black cliff, and on the northeast coast around Puerto de la Cruz. Only a few years ago, this was a small fishing village, and is now a regular stop on the international tour circuit.

About three-quarters of the island is a forest, with large areas of the interior protected from development. There is a strong and well-organized conservation movement on Tenerife, and some very strict development laws are being written. Tenerife does not discourage tourism. On the contrary, with about 1.25 million visitors a year coming to spend money, it has become a necessary part of the island economy. But the islanders are intent on maintaining a healthy economic balance between agriculture and tourism.

## **B E I N G   T H E R E**

*T*here's more to do—more sheer variety, that is—on Tenerife than on any of the other islands, so you will probably want to rent a car to cover the territory. There is, however, fairly good bus service to most major points on the island, including Mt. Teide. Bus service is frequent and inexpensive, especially in the tourist area from Puerto de la Cruz to Santa Cruz and beyond, to Playa de los Americas.

## **W H A T   T O   D O**

*A*s in the rest of the Canarias, begin with the beaches. There are excellent black- and gold-sand beaches all along the south coast, popular for windsurfing, board surfng and scuba diving. Beyond the beaches, there's deep sea fishing and sport sailing. If you want to stay on land, the island has an extensive series of hiking trails, as well as bike rentals and camping. The wildflowers are prolific on Tenerife and there are excellent opportunities for birdwatching. If you really want to get up in the air, there's hanggliding and paragliding. Beyond that, for sports, there is golf, tennis, basketball and soccer. And if you are in a reckless mood, there's always the casino in Santa Cruz.

## **W H E R E   T O   S T A Y**

*T*here is no shortage of hotel space on Tenerife, both the international tourist class and more homey hostel/pensione type establishments. See the "Where to Stay/Where to Eat" section toward the end of this book for hotel listings. Several of the hotels also offer apartments and there are many apartments for rent in Santa Cruz and Puerto de la Cruz.

## *Camping*

There are several informal camping areas and a very pleasant official campground in the hills above Garachico on the northern side of the island. This is at about a 4000 foot elevation, so take your down jacket for the evenings. It's in an area of Canary pines with several good hiking trail nearby. In forested areas outside of the national park, camping is usually permitted if you ask.

# EATING AND DRINKING

## *The Food*

There are a great many very sophisticated restaurants on Tenerife, as well as simpler, country restaurants. There are the usual wonderful fish restaurants as well as an unexpected island specialty, the restaurantes de carne, or as it is somewhat inelegantly translated, meat restaurants or barbecue restaurants. They specialize in South American style grilled meats, one more example of the close ties between the Canary Islands and South America, especially Venezuela. (We had a demonstration of this on our first visit to Tenerife; the first Canario we met, our taxi driver, had worked for many years in Venezuela, saved his money and returned to his home island to buy a house and his taxi.)

These restaurants are so popular that there is a ruta de la Carne de Los Rodeos, literally, route of the meat of Los Rodeos. This stretches from Santa Cruz, past the old airport of Los Rodeos, and well toward Tacoronte, an important wine growing center, some twelve to fourteen miles from Santa Cruz. The small village of Agua Garcia, two kilometers from Tacoronte, is lined with these restaurants. They are favorite destinations for weekend lunches or dinners and have become especially popular in recent years, as the tourist trade has brought in the cash to enable islanders to eat out more often.

Los Rodeos also offers the best airport breakfast in the world: a double espresso and two doughnuts at the old airport, now serving mostly local island flights. No idea in the world why the doughnuts are so good, but they are. They are lightly glazed with a light taste of lemon in the glaze, and perfectly cooked so they ride lightly in the tummy. Yummy!

There is an excellent daily market in Santa Cruz, called the Mercado de Nuestra Señora de Africa, which is a must-stop if you are renting an apartment during your stay, or even planning a picnic. Even if you aren't buying, a stroll through the mercado gives you a good idea of the rich abundance of vegetables and fruit available on Tenerife, where three crops of vegetables a year, including potatoes, is not unusual.

There is a strong movement on Tenerife to embrace the historical roots of the island. This becomes evident in the kitchen, where rabbit and other traditional dishes such as pork and the Guanche staple of gofio are increasingly popular, especially on holidays when more traditional meals are prepared. The one-dish meal, puchero, a stew of chicken, beef, pork, salami, garbanzos, pumpkin, cabbage and corn is a favorite on Tenerife.

## *The Wine*

In the days when Canarian wines were of major importance in the international wine market, the wines of Tenerife were generally considered of the best quality. Today, the wines of Hierro and Lanzarote are generally more highly regarded than those of Tenerife, but Tenerife's winemakers are working hard to improve that image. The chief wine centers are Tacaronte and Icod, both on the northern slope of the island.

The vines grown in small plots on terraced hillsides are pruned back so that they are very short, perhaps a foot off the ground, and are trained to form a running chain of vines. Since most of the vines grow on the cooler, northern side of

# TENERIFE

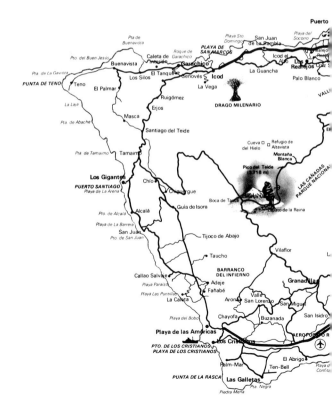

the island, the leaves are cut away, leaving the grape clusters exposed to the sun. The vineyards are 'mulched' with a layer of small volcanic stones, covered with pine needles to conserve moisture.

The major wine festival on Tenerife is November 30, the feast of St. Andrew, when the new wines are tasted with roasted chestnuts. On the eve of St. Andrew, mobs of children rush through the streets dragging strings of tin cans and making as much noise as possible to frighten away the evil spirits.

Historically, the most important grape was Malvasia. Now, red, white and rosé wines are made from several grapes, including the Palomino and a local variation called negromal. The rosé in particular can be delicious, especially when served slightly chilled with grilled fish.

There is a small wine museum in Icod on the Plaza de la Constitution, just around the corner from the famed dragon tree of Icod. The museum, called Casa Museo del Vino Malvasia, sells some of the local vintages, as well as local cheeses and handrolled Tenerife cigars. A few winemaking artifacts are on display, as are brochures and information about the local wines. The Plaza itself is a very pretty little place, with some fine examples of Canarian architecture.

There is also a ex officio wine museum in Tacoronte called Bodegas Alvaro at Calle Waque 4 (telephone: 922-56 03 59). Bodegas Alvaro is strictly a commercial enterprise, but it's worth a visit. There is a huge collection of wine displayed, some bottles full, some empty, dating from the middle of the nineteenth century. There are some fine old Tenerife malvasias for sale, the only place on the island we saw them offered. There are also current table wines in large containers.

Tenerife doesn't produce enough wine to meet local and tourist demand, but there is a good selection of Mainland wines in most restaurants. The international hotel restaurants also offer a few French and Italian wines.

There's something magical about Tenerife. You know it the moment your jet banks down toward the airport outside Santa Cruz de Tenerife and you catch a glimpse of snow-topped Mt. Teide, the peak well above the clouds. Teide is a Zen graphic, a slash of white against black volcanic rock against a blue sky, all grounded in a puffy white cloud cover with a fringe of green (the forests of Tenerife). The whole picture is framed by a blue sea.

Teide is well on view, both coming and going from the island. Coming, you think, 'I really want to get a closer look at that peak,' and going, you think, 'I really want to see it again.'

It calls you back, Teide does. You can see Teide from all of the western islands—Gomera, Hierro and La Palma—and you can see all those islands from Teide. It is significant that in the Parador on Gomera, one of the major attractions is the 'Teide Saloon,' which has a special window centered on the mountain. On La Palma, people stop their cars at special highway overlooks where Teide is on view when the day is clear.

But it isn't only Teide that makes Tenerife a special place. Sorting through memories of Tenerife, we recall several places scattered around the island that evoke a special feeling: the Mirador del Bailadero (or dancing place), which looks down on the white village of Taganana; the deep green woods around the area of Pico de Ingles; gazing out over the blue seas; the jagged black, red and beige peaks of the rim of the caldera in the Cañadas del Teide.

We are often asked which is our favorite island among the Canaries. Like a parent with several children, we always say we like them all in different ways, which is perfectly true. We wouldn't want to be without any of them. But Tenerife is truly special. Not only for its great natural beauty, but for its people. That becomes clear very soon after arrival. We always stay in Santa Cruz, returning there again and again. Santa Cruz, a city of about 200,000 inhabitants, is not the center of tourism on Tenerife, but it makes a very good base from which to explore the island. , With a busy port (the largest in Spain in tonnage handled), it is the commercial center of the islands and shares with Las Palmas de Gran Canaria the administration of the islands. The people of Santa Cruz are known throughout the islands for their friendliness and cheerfulness. And they do love to party. The Guinness Book of World Records lists the biggest dance ever held on Planet Earth as occurring on March 3, 1987, when 240,000 people took part in a pre-Lentan Carnival dance in Santa Cruz.

But there are reasons other than smiling faces and late night heavy-duty partying to stay in Santa Cruz. Now, this is difficult to explain, so pay attention. While being absolutely up-to-date with its own punk rockers, skateboarders and political demonstrations, Santa Cruz has the feeling of a Hollywood movie made in the 1940's. You know, the kind of film where the hero and heroine go walking off arm-in-arm down a dimly lit street at two in the morning with no thought of muggings or other street crimes? Well, that's the case in Santa Cruz. Despite being visited by upwards of one million tourists a year and despite being a major port city, Santa Cruz rarely has street crime. So take that for granted. You are safer on the streets of Santa Cruz than just about anywhere you could imagine.

It is an excellent city for walking, with several large parks and a pleasant tree-shaded rambla, or main thoroughfare, the Rambla del General Franco, stretching through the heart of the city. It's a fascinating walk, with several good restaurants and bars, news and flower kiosks and a number of pieces of sculpture that the city bought and left in place after an international arts exhibit centered on the Rambla and the nearby Garcia Sanbaria in 1973. A stroll up the Rambla, then down through the park makes a nice morning walk. Beyond the park, it's only a dozen or so short blocks to the port and the Plaza de España.

To the north, past the monument to the Spanish Civil War dead, the skyline is filled with the jagged peaks of the Anaga

Mountains, where there are many miles of hiking trails and informal campsites. If the day is clear, you will also be able to see the snow-covered peak of Teide, probably floating above a sea of clouds. Next to the Plaza de España is the Plaza de la Candelaria with a fine marble statue of the Virgin of Candelaria. The story goes that in 1390, two Guanche shepherds discovered a statue of the Virgin washed up on the beach at Candelaria, a small village a few miles down the coast from Santa Cruz. The Guanches worshipped the virgin as Chaxiraxi and placed her in a cave at San Blas, a few kilometers away. Dominican monks converted the local Guanches to Christianity, along with the virgin, and housed her in a new church at Candelaria, where she lived happily until she was swept to sea by a storm in 1826. A modern basilica was completed in 1958 with a copy of the original statue. In 1867, Our Lady of Candelaria was named the patroness of all the islands.

The Calle de Castillo, the main shopping street, opens out of the plaza. You can buy anything on Calle de Castillo, from good Spanish leather to cheap souvenir trinkets.

Within a few blocks of the Plaza de España are several buildings worth a closer look. In the Paso Alto Castle, you can see the cannon called the Tiger. This cannon fired the ball that took off Admiral Nelson's right arm when he attacked Santa Cruz in 1797. He lost the battle, as well.

The most important church in Santa Cruz is the Iglesia de Nuestra Señora de la Concepción with some excellent altar pieces and a remarkable tiered balcony. Near the church is the Archaeological Museum, housed on the third floor of the eighteenth century El Cabildo Insular Palace (the entrance is on Avenida Brava Murillo). It has some artifacts of Guanche life on display, as well as mummies set in their cave surroundings, a rather macabre diorama.

Well, all this walking about should have worked up an appetite. There's a snug little bar-restaurant called Bar Jabugo on the Rambla Pulido, just off the Rambla Franco. You can make a tasty lunch of tapas there with a bottle of the local rosado or a wine from the Mainland. Be sure to get an order of Palmero cheese from the island of La Palma. It's a semi-soft white cheese, slightly salty, made from a mixture of goat and sheep milk. Delicious!

·  ·  ·  ·  ·  ·  ·  ·  ·  ·  ·  ·  **SNAPSHOT**

*We were wandering a bit in the center of Santa Cruz, a few blocks up from the harbor near the Plaza de Weyler. Just killing time before dinner at the Hotel Mencey. Naturally, our thoughts turned to food and drink.*

*We were several blocks from our favorite tapas bar, so we started peering into various bars, trying to agree on one that looked promising. We eventually selected a small bar down a short flight of stairs. It served tapas, but also opened into a larger, bustling restaurant.*

*We each ordered a glass of Torres Sangre de Toro and some local cheese and olives. The service was quick and friendly, the cheese was delicious, the bread was fresh and the wine, of course, was excellent*

*We congratulated ourselves on a good choice, then looked around to discover why we had, in fact, chosen this particular place. It didn't take long to figure it out. There were older people in the bar who were perhaps retired, young couples with children, a few well-dressed men who might have been bankers just off work, and a couple of men who could have been manual laborers just off the construction site. A television was tuned to a sporting event, but the sound was off.*

*We decided then and there that the formula for finding a good tapas bar was simple: old people, young people, children, rich and poor people and no loud television.*

The nearby town of La Laguna—about six miles away—makes a good afternoon trip from Santa Cruz. In 1496, Alonso Fernández de Lugo, an Andalucian, founded Laguna making it the first capital of the archipelago. At the time, there was a small lagoon or lake nearby, which has since dried up.

In 1701, the island's first and to this point only university was founded in Laguna, and the city has that bubbling air of excitement found in many university towns. But that animation only enhances the bright, witty, Spanish sophistication of Laguna. There are bookstores, art galleries, antique shops and trendy boutiques. Laguna is not just a shopper's delight, though; there is an underlying sense of calm and peace in the city. Perhaps that relates to the historic plan of the town, which Lugo laid out on a classic grid plan, with narrow streets connecting pleasant plazas overlooked by eighteenth and nineteenth century balconied homes.

One of my favorite plazas in the islands is the Plaza del Adelantado, or governor's square. The town hall (ayuntamiento) is on one side of the plaza. It has been restored to colonial Canarian style and is quite attractive. On Sunday mornings you can buy chocolate-dipped churros in the Plaza del Adelantado, those long doughnut-like twists which taste absolutely delicious on those certain mornings when you are feeling the indulgences of the night before.

Just a few blocks down the street from the plaza is the Iglesia de la Concepción, a remarkable early sixteenth-century church with a beautifully carved Mudejar ceiling and a baroque pulpit.

Laguna is situated on the edge of the ancient *laurasilva* forest at an altitude of about 1800 feet. This is just a fragment of the ancient forest system that once covered a great deal of northern Tenerife. You can see other *laurasilva* remnants on Hierro, Gomera and La Palma. From Laguna, you can take a paved road that cuts through the heart of the mountainous Anaga headland, known locally as the Monte de las Mercedes, to El Bailadero, then back to the coast at Playa de las Teresitas. Here, you'll be near the old fishing port of San Andrés, northeast of Santa Cruz, so that you will have completed the day's loop.

Before tackling the mountains, however, it must be lunch time. A fairly early lunch could be just the ticket for a long afternoon of sightseeing. The well-known Ruta de la Carne (see "The Food" section) begins at Laguna. A ruta restaurant, El Rodeo, features meats and chicken served on a skewer. You pay a fixed price and choose what you want.

If you are interested in some delicious local foods with more variety than a carne restaurant, our favorite is Casa Tomas, a few kilometers down the road in El Socarro, toward the Mirador Pico del Ingles. Casa Tomas is a *casa comida*, a simple restaurant, family run with good, wholesome, inexpensive and plentiful food. Casa Tomas is very popular among the locals and its several rooms are often crowded. You may have to take a number and wait for a seat. There is no menu. Just ask what the day's specialties are. The servings are really large, so you might like to share two or three dishes, depending on how many are in your party. Costillas con papas, salt cured pork ribs with corn on the cob and potatoes and a parsley mojo, are a specialty that are often available, as well as a favorite of ours, carne con papas, chunks of beef stewed and topped with fried potatoes. Flavorful, crisply fried sardines, fava bean stew, mixed vegetable and lettuce salads and jugs of local wine round out the offerings. Some Spanish language skills are helpful at Casa Tomas.

The Anaga headland is a range of volcanic peaks that dominates the northeast corner of the island. There are a series of spectacular viewpoints or miradors all along the route. Happy hiker signs with smiling faces on them are posted where hiking trails cross the road. If you want to hike in the Anaga, you can pick up a map of hiking trails at the tourist office in either Laguna or Santa Cruz.

There is a rustic restaurant-bar at El Bailadero near the end of the road. The right turn leads to San Andrés, the left, to a narrow, twisting road that leads to the village of Taganana. The road to Taganana was finished only about fifteen years ago. Before that, one either walked there or rode a donkey. For the ambitious, there is a good hiking trail that leaves from just behind the restaurant to Taganana.

The view from Bailadero is breathtaking, as the entire northern shore of the island seems to fall away below the windows. It's a good place to stop for a glass of local wine (you can see the vineyards from the window, growing right to the edge of the cliffs above the sea) with some sharp goat cheese, a plate of olives and a round of the anise-flavored bread.

Bailadero is a destination point for many bicyclists who ride up either from Laguna or San Andrés. They eat a hearty lunch before coasting back downhill.

The word Bailadero means dancing place. In times of little rain (which is frequently the case on Tenerife) the Guanches would gather there to dance and pray for rain. They would also drive mother goats to the spot, leaving the kids down in the valley. The theory was that the bleating of the goats would call the attention of the gods to their rain dances.

After the conquest, El Bailadero had an reputation for centuries as an evil dancing place for witches. But after the Tenerifos learned that foreigners like to drive, hike or bike long distances for the view, they didn't hesitate to establish a restaurant to ease the appetite of the hungry viewers.

The drive down to the coast is very pretty, as well as educational. You leave the green forested zone and pass almost at once into the typical semi-arid desert landscape of the island's south, where rain is scantier than in the north. Near San Andrés is the Playa de las Tresitas, a kind of monument to a former mayor of San Andrés who decided to create a new industry for his small town. Noting that the nearby city of Santa Cruz was lacking in beaches, he arranged to have sand brought from Africa to make a white-sand beach, carefully protected by breakwaters. His scheme seems to be working; a lively marina has sprung up on the Playa with boats for charter and rental shops for windsurfing, sailing and diving.

If your timing is right, you will be back in Santa Cruz in time for dinner at one of the city's many fine restaurants, like Coto de Antonio. The clubby feel of this side street restaurant is more like Madrid than Tenerife. This very comfortable restaurant offers good food at moderate prices. The house salad comes with a sharply flavored, delicious green sauce of minced parsley and garlic, chopped egg white and capers, vinegar and olive oil. Brochetto de Solomillo con Riñones, skewered, grilled beef fillet with kidneys, was perfectly cooked, with both meats still pink and tender.

There are several different approaches to Mt. Teide and the locals can spend a good deal of time discussing which is the best. Four roads lead to the Cañadas plateau below the peak—from there, a cable car can carry you to the summit. There is also a hiking trail to the peak and a hostel with overnight accomodations. Check for reservations at the Tourist Office in Santa Cruz or Laguna, as it is often filled. It's a favorite overnight excursion of the locals, who like to climb to the iron cross that marks the summit to watch the sunset in the evening, and then to get up early and watch the sunrise next day.

The favorite route for locals starts from La Esperenza, just outside Laguna. The road, known as the Carretera Dorsal, climbs the ridge of the Anaga mountains that divide the island, giving good views of Santa Cruz and Laguna. In a few kilometers, the road winds through Pinar de la Esperenza, a thick forest of Canary pines.

If you want a moment or two of history, there is a clearing in the woods and a monument to Franco at Las Raices, where the general met with his staff to begin the coup against the government in Madrid in 1936. Earlier in the year, the Popular Front of the Spanish Republic had exiled Franco to the Canaries and made him Captain-General of the islands. We were told that the monument is often vandalized, which is hardly surprising, if a bit beside the point by this time and in that place.

A bit further on is a mirador, Pico de las Flores Belvedere, which offers a sweeping panorama of the north and south coasts and the Laguna basin. It's a graphic view of the green fertility of the north and the semi-desert landscape of the south.

Beyond the mirador, the road comes to a pass, which is the beginning of the remarkable volcanic plateau of Las Cañadas del Teide. Here, an ancient volcano collapsed into a caldera about three million years ago, before giving birth to Teide. The caldera is about ten miles wide.

There are several viewpoints on the road, as well as some inviting roadside bar-restaurants, where you can have an espresso or a glass of wine on the terrace with good views of the amazing plateau. If it is a sunny day (and the Cañadas are sometimes fogged in), you can see an amazing variety of colors and hues in the rocks where minerals have been stratified by volcanic action.

There is an easy, level hike that lasts three to four hours, depending on your speed, and starts at the Nuestra Señora de las Nieves, a small church near the Parador and a popular tourist destination called Los Roques. The hike winds through the Cañadas back toward El Portillo. Along the way, you can see the stone huts that the Guanches first built as summer shelter for shepherds who brought their sheep into caldera to graze. The huts have been in use for centuries. May is the most spectacular time for wildflowers, including endemic species of violets and daisies and a pink broom, the retama del pico.

If you begin the hike in mid-morning, you'll have a good appetite for a hearty late lunch at the Parador. Try to get a window with a view of Teide and give yourself enough time to enjoy a leisurely lunch, because the Parador specializes in Canarian dishes and does an excellent job. They have some local wines on the list, as well as a good selection of Mainland wines. After dessert, try a glass of the Parador's homemade liqueur, a rue-flavored marc called *parra*.

Potaje de Berros con Piña de Maiz is a local specialty at

the Parador. This stew of white beans, watercress, corn on the cob, potatoes and bits of pork is a welcome warmth after the often chilly heights of Teide.

It is possible to map out a one-day circle of the island, but it would be much more enjoyable to stretch it to at least two days and preferably more. Beginning in Santa Cruz in the early morning, you will easily arrive in Puerto de la Cruz in time for a mid-morning espresso on a seaside terrace overlooking the rocky shore where a number of natural swimming pools have been designed by the Canarian one-man art band, César Manrique. The complex of pools called Lago de Martiánez is an amazing creation.

As you sip your coffee (why not with a little brandy or anise—after all, you are on vacation), you'll likely hear a linguistic potpourri of Spanish, English, German, French, Swedish and Danish. Puerto is one of the top international resorts, and it's easy to see why. Despite greeting upwards of one million tourists annually, it shares with Santa Cruz an open, friendly feeling. The waiters smile, the shopkeepers are helpful and the coffee is good.

Puerto is, in fact, an intriguing blend of the very modern and the traditional Spanish fishing village. Highrises cuddle cheek-to-cheek with fishermen's houses and bustling modern shopping streets suddenly open up on a charming Spanish plaza. There's also an outstanding botanical garden with an international collection of over 4000 plants, plus thousands of local birds, as well as more exotic parrots.

In sum, Puerto de la Cruz has gracefully made the transition from a quiet village to a modern tourist resort. It's a good place to hang out.

Only a few kilometers inland is the lovely town of La Orotava, from which the surrounding valley takes its name. The town was an important center for the Guanches who lived in great numbers in the fertile valley. They called the town Taoro and it was said to be the richest of the nine Guanche kingdoms of Tenerife.

Colonial La Orotava developed around the Iglesia de Nuestra Señora de la Concepción, which was first built in the sixteenth century. The church was destroyed by earthquakes early in the eighteenth century, although the stunning high altar (made in marble by the Italian sculptor Gagini) was rescued when the present structure was built in the late eighteenth century. The church has a fine baroque façade between twin towers.

The oldest church on Tenerife is the Iglesia de Santiago, which dates to 1498. The church is located in nearby Los Realejos, where the Guanche chiefs finally surrendered to the Spanish in 1496.

There are also outstanding examples of eighteenth century domestic architecture. Many houses have highly polished Canarian balconies. On the Calle de San Francisco, two of these have been arranged as tourist centers/museums and are worth a visit. A nonworking, eighteenth century winery has been set up on the patio of Casa de los Balcones at number three Calle de San Francisco with a giant press and other state-of-the-art 1700's winemaking machinery. The Casa de los Balcones also has a particularly fine selection of local lacework.

There is good lacework to be found on all of the islands, with each island having its own particular pattern or style. The best-known style on Tenerife is called Galleta. If you are in luck, a laceworking class may be in progress. If so, visitors are allowed to watch the work being done, often by young women in traditional Tenerife costumes.

Across the street is another crafts house cum museum called La Casa del Turista, which was originally a convent built in the sixteenth century. It has a marvelous terrace looking out over the Orotava valley. On the terrace, there is a display of the sand and pebble paintings, which are made in the main plaza every year for the feast of Corpus Christi. The streets leading to the plaza are strewn with flowers, which remain in place until the Sunday following Corpus Christi, when the romeria (pilgrimage) of San Isidroe occurs.

Everyone from the valley who works on the land joins a procession through the town—often wearing traditional costumes and riding or leading bullock carts.

A good overlook above the town is named the Mirador Humboldt after the German botanist Alexander Von Humboldt, who wrote a book about the botany of the islands. This is the same fellow for whom the Humboldt current in the North Pacific and Humboldt County in California are named. From the mirador, the whole valley spreads out below you, a vista which was once all dragon trees. The dragon tree, an unusual tree of the lily family which yields "dragon's blood" or a red juice when the bark is scraped, was sacred to the Guanches. In the eighteenth and early nineteenth centuries, most of these long-lived trees were cut down to make room for banana plantations, which are now giving way to housing developments.

Perhaps the most famous dragon tree on Tenerife (there are a few dragons on the nearby islands of La Palma, Gomera, Hierro and Gran Canaria) is in the wine town of Icod, west of La Orotava on the island's north coast. A thriving cottage industry has sprung up around a dragon tree there, believed to be at least 2500 years old. It is difficult to find the exact age of the dragons, because they do not have growth rings. Age can only be determined by counting the branches, but this is obviously an imprecise method, since branches do break off. But whatever its exact age, the Icod dragon is an impressive site. Viewed from certain angles, it is framed by several palm trees with a view of Teide in the far background.

This particular dragon was an object of great veneration to the Guanches, who regarded the trees as fertility symbols. More practically, they made shields from the bark of the tree and used the red resin as a medicine and a fluid with which to embalm the dead. The blood of the dragon was also used in the seventeenth century to dye hair, to stain marble and to varnish musical instruments.

A few kilometers beyond Icod (which comes from the

Guanche word, benicod, meaning beautiful place), is the little seaside town of Garachico. This was Tenerife's most important port until it was almost destroyed by an eruption of Teide in 1706. Now, it's a pleasant tourist destination with several good restaurants, a home-based cigar factory and a stimulating series of natural swimming pools. These pools are really corridors—often no more than four or five feet wide—through the seaside ancient volcanic flow. When the tide is in, the pools fill. Gently awash in the oncoming breakers, they are good places to swim.

There is excellent scuba diving all along this coast, especially off Garachico. Chartered boats from Puerto de la Cruz often sail here.

One of the best places for lunch on the north coast is back at Icod at the Restaurant Carmen, a lively café with terraced gardens perched on a cliff overlooking the sea. Although Carmen specializes in seafood (which is appropriate, since Carmen is the Spanish patroness of the sea), one of our favorite dishes there is the Papas Rellenas con Carne. The potatoes are stuffed with meat, topped with a white sauce and baked. Tasty and satisfying. These make a good first course followed by Carmen's delicious fried mackerel, Caballas, served, of course, with more potatoes and mojos. Bacalao encebollado, salt cod stewed with lots of onions in a thinnish red pepper sauce, is good. The cod is rather tough, but the sauce is great.

The island's south coast is a beach lovers' bonanza, with a series of resorts reaching almost from Santa Cruz right around the tip of the island to Playa de las Americas. There are some very tasteful tourist developments along the way. One fantastic golden-sand beach, Playa del Médano, is one of the best windsurfing beaches in the world. On the west coast of the island, the rhythm and pace of life change. It's still tourist territory, but much less visited than the south coast.

There is a superb hike at the village of Adeje, which sits up in the hills above the coast in a canyon called the Barranco

*168*

del Infierno, or Hell's Canyon. It's a deep ravine, so deep the locals say the sun never shines on the bottom. It is also a botanist's paradise. The path through the gorge cuts back and forth across a narrow stream, choked with willows and eucalypti. There is a feeling of great isolation and wilderness in the Barranco, although you are only a few miles from the roaring tourist beaches of the coast.

A bit further north, you'll come to Puerto de Santiago. Santiago has an excellent black-sand beach and is a good place to charter boats for deep sea fishing or scuba diving. The town marina has more than 300 moorings and there is almost always a boat available.

Beyond Santiago, the countryside is more remote, with a number of charming and unvisited villages, where one can have long, delicious lunches in tiny roadside cafes, often with views of Teide and the sea. There are several good hikes along the headland here (inquire locally at Teno Alto or Masca) with sweeping views of the Atlantic, Mt. Teide and back down the coast to the highrises of Playa de las Américas.

It is entirely possible to lose yourself for days in this unspoiled district. You can usually find a room for rent, even in the tiny villages. If not, you can always drop back down to the coast and find rooms at Playa de Santiago or Buenavista, a bit further north.

That is one of the great charms, not only of Tenerife, but of all the Canaries—that feeling of isolation, of somehow stepping back into the eighteenth century, while being only a few minutes' drive from the luxury of civilization.

One is free to indulge one's mood in the Canaries, indeed, to indulge in all the pleasures of the Canaries.

## *Useful Information*

Tourist Offices
   Avenida José Antonio 2, Santa Cruz: 922-24 25 92
   Plaza de la Iglesia 3, Puerto de la Cruz: 922-38 60 00

San Eugenio, Pueblo Canario, Playa de las Américas: 922-79 33 12

Avenida del Gran Poder, La Laguna: 922-54 08 10

Bicycle Rentals

Autos y Motos Rueda, Calle Obispo Pérez Cáceres 2, Puerto de la Cruz: 922-38 29 02

Italia Chic, Centro Commercial El Presidente, Playa de las Américas: 922-79 66 27

Hiking

Federacion de Montañismo, Calle San Sebastian 76, Santa Cruz: 922-22 67 71

Interpretation Service, Teide National Park: 922-25 99 03. This is a private guide service that leads hikes into the park.

Sailing and Windsurfing

Escuela de Vela, Puerto Colón, Playa de las Américas: 922 75 19 88

Hotel Windsurf (a four-star hotel), Escuela Sun-Wind, El Médano: 922-75 19 88. (The El Médano is generally considered to be one of the best beaches in the world for windsurfing. We first heard of it from our accountant in California.)

Diving

Puerto de Santiago Marina: 922-86 7179. Rentals for both diving and deep sea fishing.

Club Barracuda, Hotel Paraiso Floral: 922-78 07 25

Club Poseidon, Ten Bel: 922-73 01 32

Club Sarpentin, Hotel Las Palmeras, Playa de las Américas: 922-75 27 08

Rolf Max Schweizer, Calle El Pino 45, Los Gigantes: 922-86 72 57

Golf

Amarilla Golf, Apartado No. 8-38620, San Miguel de Abona: 922-78 57 77

Club de Golf el Peñon, Apartado No. 125, La Laguna: 922-25 02 40

Golf del Sur, El Guincho, San Miguel de Abona: 922-17 62 46

TENERIFE

# RECIPES

The cuisine of the Canary Islands is simple and healthful, based on the freshest of seafood and produce from the garden and orchard. The food is satisfying because of the intense flavors of the mojo sauces that accompany almost every meal.

Those wishing an international cuisine can find it on almost all the islands, everything from British pub grub to Italian pizzas to Chinese fried rice.

But we would urge a serious exploration of the Canarian kitchen, where cooks have taken elements from Mainland Spain and the Americas, to create a unique cuisine.

The local table wines should also be explored. They can be quite good in a simple, straight-forward way. It is the magnificent dessert wines that deserve an especially close tasting.

And, of course, the delicious wines of the Mainland are available everywhere.

## MOJO

Mojos are the secret sauces of the Canary Islands. They show up on your table in as many variations of ingredients as the seasons produce.

The sauces vary in their intensity of spice and heat

according to the cook's taste. A restaurant will usually present two mojos, one red and one green. The main ingredient can be cilantro, green pepper, parsley, red peppers or tomatoes. The mojos taste great with salad, steamed vegetables, boiled potatoes, grilled fish and meats and with bread when you dunk it. They are simple, quickly prepared and add new dimensions to the foods they accompany. The lightness of the mojos fits perfectly into today's lifestyle. So get your mojo working.

## Mojo Rojo
Red sauce

I particularly like this mojo with grilled pork.

*1 ancho chile*
*1 cup cilantro leaves*
*3 cloves garlic*
*4 sprigs fresh thyme, leaves only*
*1/2 teaspoon salt*
*1/4 teaspoon ground cumin*
*1/2 cup olive oil*
*2 tablespoons red wine vinegar*

Put the chile in a bowl and pour boiling water over it. Cover and let rest 10 minutes.

Take the chile out of the water. Remove the stem and seeds, but do not peel.

Combine the chile, cilantro, garlic, thyme, salt and cumin in the food processor. With the motor running, combine and add the oil, vinegar and water.

## Mojo Verde
Green sauce

*5 medium-sized cloves of garlic, peeled*
*l bunch Italian leafy parsley, about l cup leaves*
*1/2 cup olive oil*
*1 tablespoon red wine vinegar*
*1/4 cup water*
*1/4 teaspoon each salt and freshly ground black*
pepper

In a blender or food processor, purée the garlic and parsley. With the motor running, mix and gradually add the oil and vinegar. Season with the salt and pepper. Taste and adjust as needed.

Serve immediately. This sauce is best when freshly made. It will turn gray if refrigerated until the next day.

## Salsa Aguacate
Avocado mayonnaise

Makes about 2 cups of sauce.

*l extra large egg*
*l large clove garlic*
*l large Haas avocao*
*3 tablespoons freshly squeezed lemon juice*
*1/2 cup each olive oil and corn oil*
*1/2 teaspoon salt*
*dash of cayenne*

In a blender or food processor purée the egg with the garlic. Add the avocado and lemon juice and purée. With the motor running, combine and gradually add the oils. Season with the salt and cayenne.

Let rest 30 minutes before serving.

Variation:

Chop and fold 1/2 cup cilantro leaves into the finished sauce.

### *Churros de Pescado*

Fish fritters

Serves 6 as a tapa

*3 cloves garlic*
*2 tablespoons parsley*
*3 extra large eggs*
*1/4 lb. fish such as snapper or fresh cod filets*
*1 cup boiling water*
*1/2 teaspoon salt*
*1 cup all purpose white flour*
*olive oil for deep frying*
*coarse salt*

In a food processor whirl the garlic, parsley and eggs until thick. Add the fish and blend until smooth. In a small saucepan bring the water and salt to a boil. Stir in the flour all at once and keep stirring until the mixture forms a ball and pulls away from the sides of the pan. Add the ball of dough to the fish in the food processor and whirl to combine.

Pour one inch of oil into a pan or skillet. Or use

a deep fryer or an electric skillet that will keep the temperature even. Heat the oil to 375º. Drop a bit of dough into the hot oil. The oil is ready for frying when the dough gently descends into the oil and immediately but gently rises to the surface. If the dough sinks too fast, that means the oil is too hot; if it stays submerged too long, the oil must not be hot enough and the churros will be soggy.

Put the churros mixture into a pasty bag fitted with a fluted tube. Hold the bag over the pan and squeeze the dough into the hot oil. Cut the dough off into 3" lengths or curl the dough into rings and cut it off.

Do not crowd the pan. Remove the churros when they are puffed and golden. Repeat with the remaining dough.

Sprinkle with coarse salt and serve immediately with a crisp white wine, such as Torres Viña Sol.

## *Pan Con Anis*

Canarian bread with anise

We found this bread on all the islands, but I think the best came from Gomera, where I got this version. If you have your own favorite white bread recipe, simply add a teaspoon of dried anise seeds.

*4 1/2 cups white unbleached flour*
*1 1/2 cups of water*
*1 tablespoon yeast*
*1 teaspoon salt*
*1 teaspoon anise*
*1 tablespoon olive oil*

Add the yeast to one cup of warm water and 2 cups of flour. Stir together and let stand about one hour until the mixture or sponge doubles in size. Add 2 more cups of flour, about 1/2 cup of water, salt, anise and olive oil. Knead for about ten minutes, working about 1/2 cup of flour into the dough. Shape into a freeform loaf or put in bread pan and allow to rise another hour until double in size. Put in cold oven set at 400º and bake for 45 minutes.

## Potaje de Berros Con Piña de Maiz
Watercress soup with corn on the cob
Serves 6 to 8

We had this delicious dish at the parador on Tenerife while gazing at the snow-capped peak of Mt. Teide.

Begin preparation the day before.

*12 oz. great northern white beans*
*1-1/2 lb. hambock—have butcher crack it into several pieces*
*2 bay leaves*
*l large bunch of chopped watercress, washed , root ends removed*
*2 ears of corn, shucked, cut into 1-1/2" chunks*
*l lb. unpeeled tiny red new potatoes, whole*
*l teaspoon salt*
*1/2 teaspoon freshly ground black pepper*

Put the beans into a large pot and cover abundantly with cold water. Soak them overnight.

Drain the beans and return them to the pot. Add more water until the water is 2" above the beans. Add the hamhock and bay leaves. Bring to a boil, reduce heat and cook until the beans are tender—about 1 hour.

Take the hamhock out of the pot, remove the bones and cut the meat into small pieces. Return the meat to the beans and discard the skin and bones. Add the watercress, corn, potatoes, salt and pepper. Increase the heat and bring to a boil. Reduce the heat and cook until the potatoes and corn are tender. Taste to adjust salt.

Serve hot in big soup bowls.


## *Potaje de Lentejas*
Potatoes and lentils
Serves 6 to 8

This is a standard soup of the islands.

*1 lb. lentils, washed*
*1 onion, minced*
*2 tomatoes, finely chopped*
*2 bay leaves*
*1 lb. potatoes, peeled, cut into 1" cubes*
*3/4 lb. chorizo, cut into 1" thick rounds if firm, or left whole if soft*
*1/2 lb. cubed pork loin*
*8 cloves garlic*
*1/4 cup parsley leaves*

*1/2 teaspoon cumin seeds, toasted in a dry skillet until they "dance"*
*1 teaspoon paprika*
*1/2 teaspoon freshly ground black pepper*
*2 teaspoon salt*

Put the lentils, onions, tomatoes and bay leaves into a large soup pot. Cover with 8 cups of cold water. Bring the water to a boil, reduce heat and cook for 30 minutes. Add the potatoes, chorizo and the pork to the pot. If you are using soft chorizos, add them whole. Before serving, remove them, slice them, and return them to the potaje.

Grind the remaining ingredients together with a mortar and pestle or in a blender. Stir the paste into the potaje. Cook for about 45 minutes or until the lentils and potatoes are tender.

Taste for salt and add more if necessary.

Serve hot in soup bowls with some anise flavored Canarian bread.

## Sancocho

Salt cod and potatoes in a green sauce

This traditional recipe would be served with a bowl of gofio moistened with some of the cooking liquid. The thick paste would then be eaten with each mouthful of sancocho.

Serves 6

Begin preparation 24 hours in advance.

*1 lb. boneless, skinless salt cod*
*2 lbs. small red new potatoes, peeled*
*3 cloves garlic*
*1 chile serrano*
*1/4 cup Italian parsley leaves*
*1/4 cup cilantro leaves*
*3 tablespoons olive oil*
*2 tablespoons red wine vinegar*
*salt to taste*

Put the cod in a bowl and cover with cold water. Cover and refrigerate. Pour off the water and cover with fresh water several times in the next 24 hours. Drain the cod and discard the water.

Leave the potatoes whole unless they are quite large. Cover the potatoes with salted water. Bring the water to a boil. Continue to boil for 10 minutes.

Cut the fish into chunks about the same size as the potatoes and add to the potatoes. Cook another 10 minutes or until the potatoes are tender. Drain the fish and potatoes, reserving the cooking liquid. Put the fish and potatoes on a serving platter. Cover them to keep them warm while preparing the sauce.

In the food processor or blender grind together the garlic, chile, parsley and cilantro. Add 2 of the cooked potatoes and purée. With the motor running combine and add the oil and vinegar. Taste for salt and adjust if necessary. Add a little of the reserved cooking liquid to make a smooth sauce. Pour the sauce over the potatoes and fish and serve immediately.

## *Mejillones con Mojo Verde*
Steamed mussels with green pepper sauce

We had this delicious dish at a beachfront restaurant, Casa Juan, in the town of Caleta del Cotillo on Fuerteventura. One of those informal places where you can walk into the kitchen and sniff the soup pots, then point to the fresh fish you'd like.

Serves 6 as an entrée, more as a tapa

*48 medium sized mussels*
*1 cup dry white wine or water*
*2 large green peppers, stemed and seeded and cut into chunks*
*3 cloves garlic, peeled*
*1/2 cup parsley*
*1 very small serrano chile, stemmed and seeded*
*1/2 teaspoon salt*
*1/2 cup olive oil*
*2 tablespoons white wine vinegar*

Wash the mussels well and remove their beards with a pair of scissors.

Put the wine or water in a large lidded pot and bring to a boil. Add the mussels, cover and steam until the mussels open. Check after 5 minutes and remove any that have opened. After all the mussels have opened, strain the cooking liquid through cheesecloth into another saucepan. Cook over high heat to reduce to 2 tablespoons.

Meanwhile, in a food processor, grind together the green pepper, garlic, parsley and chile. Combine and add the 2 tablespoons cooking liquid, olive oil and vinegar. Season with salt to taste. Set aside.

Remove the top shell of the mussels and discard. Loosen each mussel from its shell, then return it to the shell. Arrange on a large platter or on individual plates. Top each mussel with some of the mojo.

Serve immediately or refrigerate, covered, and serve cold.

## Conejo en Salmorejo
Marinated rabbit

Begin preparation 24 hours ahead.
Serves 4 to 6

*2 1/2 lbs. fresh rabbit, cut into serving pieces*
*1 head of garlic, peeled*
*1/4 teaspoon cumin seeds*
*3 sprigs fresh oregano*
*1 bay leaf, spine removed*
*3 sprigs fresh parsley*
*1 tablespoon paprika*
*1/4 teaspoon each salt and freshly ground black pepper*
*1 cup dry white wine*
*2 tablespoons red wine vinegar*
*2 tablespoons olive oil*

Put the rabbit pieces into a nonreactive glass or stainless steel flat-bottomed dish so that the pieces can be easily covered by the marinade.

With a blender, mortar or food processor grind

together the garlic, cumin, oregano, bay leaf, parsley, paprika and salt and pepper. Combine with the wine and vinegar and pour this marinade over the rabbit pieces. Cover and refrigerate overnight.

Take the rabbit out of the refrigerator one hour before cooking. Remove the rabbit from the marinade. Using your hands, strip off and reserve all marinade. Pat the rabbit dry with paper towels.

Heat the olive oil in a large nonreactive skillet. Cook the rabbit quickly until golden. Pour off any excess oil and add the reserved marinade. Bring to a boil, reduce heat and cook for 30 minutes.

Serve immediately with plain boiled rice.

## *Carne Con Papas*
Meat 'n potatoes

This may look like beef stew topped with French fries and basically it is, but it's real good! This dish is very popular with the natives and is served in the casas comidas, working people's restaurants.

Serves 6

*2 lbs. boneless stew beef cut into 1" cubes*
*1 tablespoon olive oil*
*1 large onion, minced*
*1 head garlic, peeled*
*1 sweet red pepper, stemmed and seeded*
*1 cup dry white wine*
*1 teaspoon paprika*
*1/2 teaspoon each salt and freshly ground black pepper*

2 lbs. Idaho potatoes, peeled and cut into 1/2"
*sticks*
  *oil for frying*

Pat the meat dry. Heat the olive oil in a skillet and
cook the beef cubes until browned. Remove the beef
with a slotted spoon. Add the onion to the skillet and
stir to coat with the oily juices. Cook for 5 minutes over
medium heat. In food processor or blender grind the
garlic and red pepper together and stir into the
onions. Pour the wine into the onion mixture and
bring to a boil. Return the beef and any juices to the
skillet, reduce the heat, cover and cook for 30
minutes.

Meanwhile, heat 2" of oil in a pan and fry the
potatoes until golden. Remove the potatoes and
drain on paper towels. Sprinkle with salt.

Uncover the meat, increase the heat and cook to
thicken and reduce the juices. Serve the fried
potatoes on top of the meat.

## *Tarta de Cebollas y Almejas Con Queso del Hierro*

Onion tart with clams and cheese from Hierro

The cheeses of Hierro are my favorites among the
islands. They are often lighly smoked, sharp and
nutty. An unusual pairing of seafood and cheese in
this tart is absolutely delicious with the sweetness of
the carmelized onions.

Serves 8

Tart crust:
*l cup all purpose flour*
*1/4 teaspoon salt*
*1/2 cup lard ( yes, lard—use butter if you must, but the flavor will suffer!)*
*1/3 cup ice water*

Filling:
*1/3 cup olive oil*
*5 medium yellow onions, peeled and thinly sliced*
*l teaspoon salt*
*1 teaspoon freshly ground black pepper*
*1/3 cup chicken broth or dry red wine*
*1/2 lb. shelled clams\**
*1/2 cup grated sharp cheese such as asiago or a lightly smoked provolone*

(\*Fresh, shelled clams are available at many sea-food markets. The best flavor will be from fresh clams that you steam open so that you have 1/2 lb. of the clam meat. As a last resort, use canned clams.)

Preheat oven to 425º.
Put the flour and salt into a deep bowl. With two knives or a pasty cutter add the lard until it is well distributed and has formed lumps the size of gravel. Toss the mixture with a fork while adding the ice water. Quickly gather the dough into a bowl. Lay it on a lighly floured work surface. Flour the rolling pin and gently roll the dough into a 12" circle.
Have a 10" removable rim tart pan ready. Put the circle of dough into the pan and turn under any edges that extend above the rim of the pan. Cover the

dough with waxed paper and weight with dry beans or pastry weights. Bake blind—with the weights in place—for 15 minutes. Carefully lift the paper to remove the weights. Return the tart shell to the oven and cook 10 minutes longer until golden and crisp. Remove from the oven and set aside.

Meanwhile prepare the filling. Heat the olive oil in a large skillet, add the onions, sprinkle with the salt and pepper and cook slowly over low heat until the onions are really soft and golden. This may take 30 minutes. Stir in the stock or wine and cook quickly until the onions are dry.

Pile the onions into the cooked tart shell. Top with the clams. Sprinkle the top of the tart with the grated cheese. Return the tart to the oven for 5 minutes or until the cheese melts.

Serve hot from the oven or at room temperature.

## *Papas Rellenas de Carne*
Meat stuffed new potatoes

Warm, delicious and wonderfully satisfying, these homey potatoes will always remind me of Dragon trees. We had this dish for lunch, just down the hill from a splendid example of this prehistoric looking tree on the island of Tenerife.

Serves 6 as a main course or more as a tapa

*18 medium-sized red new potatoes or yellow Finnish potatoes*

*3/4 lb. ground veal or beef (or use ground turkey or chicken)*

*l medium small onion, minced*
*2 cloves garlic, minced*
*2 tablespoons parsley, minced*
*1 teaspoon salt*
*1/2 teaspoon freshly ground black pepper*
*l cup green olives, unpitted*
*l tablespoon butter*
*l 1/2 tablespoons flour*
*l cup milk*
*fresh nutmeg*
*1/2 cup grated asiago or parmesan*

Boil the potatoes whole in salted water until fork-tender. Do not overcook or the potatoes will fall apart in their later cooking. Drain the potatoes, reserving 2/3 cup of the water. Using the larger end of a melon baller, scoop out the tops of the potatoes.

Preheat oven to 375º.

Chop the scooped out parts of the potatoes and combine with the veal, onions, garlic, parsley, 1/2 teaspoon salt and 1/4 teaspoon pepper. Stuff this mixture into the potatoes and arrange closely in a baking dish. Use all the filling, mounding it on top of the potatoes. Scatter the olives around the potatoes. Pour the reserved potato water around the potatoes.

To prepare the white sauce, melt the butter in a saucepan. Stir in the flour and cook for one minute. Pour in the cold milk all at once and stir over medium heat until thickened. Season with the remaining salt and pepper and a grating of fresh nutmeg.

Drizzle the sauce over the potatoes. Sprinkle with the cheese and bake for 30 minutes.

Serve the potatoes hot with the cooking juices .

# *Flan de Arroz Con Miel*
rice flan with honey

Serves 8

*2 cups water*
*1 cup short grain white rice*
*1/2 teaspoon salt*
*zest of one lemon*
*1/4 teaspoon ground cinnamon*
*1 cup milk*
*1/2 cup sugar*
*4 large eggs, beaten*
*good quality honey*

Bring the water to a boil, add the rice, salt and cinnamon and return to a boil. Reduce the heat, cover and cook for 15 minutes. Remove from the heat. Stir in the cold milk and allow to cool.

Preheat oven to 375º.

Meanwhile, carmelize the sugar. Heat the sugar in a small heavy bottomed skillet or pan. Cook the sugar until it melts and turns a medium-dark caramel color. You need to watch the sugar closely during this process. It can burn easily. Handle it carefully, as well, because it sugar is incredibly hot and will burn you and stick to you if you touch it.

Quickly pour the caramel into 8 one-half cup flan molds or into a 4 to 5 cup ring mold. Lift the molds with a gloved hand and tilt to coat the insides. The sugar will harden very fast, so work quickly.

Stir the beaten eggs into the rice mixture. Divide

it among the molds or pour all of it into the ring mold.

Put the molds into a larger container and add enough hot water to the large container to come halfway up the sides of the molds. This large pot of water is called a *Baño Maria*, or Mary's bath.

Put the whole set-up into the preheated oven for 20 to 30 minutes or until firm.

Remove from the oven and allow to cool, or immediately run a knife around the edge of the flans and invert on dessert plates to serve hot. I prefer this flan warm, since it seems to soak up the honey more when warm, but some like it better at room temperature. Either way it's very good, but do not serve it icy cold from the refrigerator.

To serve, pass a bowl of honey around with the flans. Without the honey, the flans are not sweet enough, so encourage a generous use of honey.

## *Frangollo*
Polenta dessert with almonds and raisins

We enjoyed this old fashioned dessert on Lanzarote in a restaurant/museum that the artist César Manrique designed and dedicated to the working people of the island. Frangollo is a very popular Canarian dessert, available as a mix in stores on all the islands. But why buy a mix when it is so easy to prepare? I really love the flavors here.

> *1 quart milk*
> *1 cinnamon stick*
> *peel of one lemon*

*1/2 cup sugar*
*1 cup polenta*
*1/4 cup whole almonds, chopped*
*1/4 cup raisins*
*2 tablespoons butter*

In a heavy bottomed saucepan, combine the milk, cinnamon stick and lemon peel. Cook over the lowest possible heat. Do not let the mixture boil. Cook for about 10 minutes. Discard the cinnamon and lemon peel.

Stir in the sugar. Over low heat, gradually add the polenta, stirring constantly. Cook until the polenta thickens, about 10 minutes.

Stir in the almonds, raisins and butter.

Pour into a buttered bread pan and smooth the top. Leave to cool.

The mixture will become very firm.

To serve, turn out of the pan onto a serving platter. Cut into slices and serve cold. On Lanzarote, this was served to us with a topping of sweetened condensed milk. I prefer a dab of sour cream or a purée of fresh fruit.

Variation:

Slice the frangollo and cook slices in hot butter or olive oil until golden. Serve hot with or without a sauce.

## Bienmesabe

It tastes good to me

And so it does. I don't know whether this name originated out of defensiveness or arrogance, but this dessert, sauce, candy, or whatever, is wildly popular and can even be bought in jars at roadside stands. We encountered it most often on La Palma .

Try it as a sauce on vanilla ice cream, with fresh fruit or perhaps as a filling for a plain cake.

> *l 1/2 cups whole almonds*
> *2 cups water*
> *2 cups sugar*
> *4 egg yolks*
> *10 Marie biscuits*

Preheat oven to 400º.

Spread the almonds on a baking sheet and toast in the oven for 12 minutes. Remove the almonds and finely grind them in a blender or food processor. Transfer the almonds to a bowl.

Combine the water and sugar in a heavy bottomed saucepan. Bring to a boil and cook rapidly for 8 minutes or until the mixture reaches 225º on a candy thermometer.

Meanwhile, beat the egg yolks in the food processor until thick.

With the motor of the processor on, gradually add the hot syrup. Whirl in the almond mixture.

Break up the biscuits in a bowl. Pour the almond mixture over them. Let rest at room temperature for 4 hours before serving.

Variations:

1. Use Italian style amaretto cookies instead of the Marie biscuits.

2. Leave out the cookies all together and use the almond mixture as a sauce.

. . . . . . . . . . . . . **SNAPSHOT**

*Potaje Canario, Puchero Canario and Rancho Canario. These three dishes crop up alone or together on menus on all the islands. The ingredients for each are very similar: potatoes, cabbage, beans or lentils, meat, corn on the cob. The potaje has more broth than solids. The puchero is served in two courses: meat and vegetables first, with a mojo and the broth following. Gofio is stirred in to make it thicker. The rancho has more meat than vegetables, has a yellow tinge to the stock and is a bit more stewlike. Sometimes the gofio is just mixed with enough of the broth to form a paste and is eaten with the fingers .*

# WHERE TO STAY, WHERE TO EAT

Not all of the hotels and restaurants listed here have been personally visited by the authors, but they do come highly recommended by Canarians. ·For longer stays, check the tourist offices for lists of apartments, pensiones and other, less expensive accommodations. The restaurants listed here are the cream of the crop, but it is hard to find a bad meal in the Canaries. Let your nose be your guide.

## LANZAROTE
(928 is the telephone code for the entire island. You need not dial it when calling on the island.)

*Hotels*

### Five Stars
Hotel Salinas, Ave. de las Islas, Costa Teguise: 590 420
Hotel Jameso Playa, Playa de los Pocillos, Puerto del Carmen: 826 405

### Four Stars
Hotel Oasis, Ave. del Mar, Costa Teguise: 590 410
Hotel Teguise Playa, Ave. del Jubilado, Costa Teguise: 810 979
Hotel La Galea, Ave. del Jubilado, Costa Teguise: 590 550
Hotel Lanzarote Garden, Ave. de las Islas, Costa Teguise: 590 063

Hotel Los Zocos, Ave. de Las Islas, Costa Teguise: 81 58 17
Hotel Puerto Tahiche, Calle Teguise, Costa Teguise: 59 01 17
Hotel Lanzarote Beach Club, Ave. de las Islas, Costa Teguise:
81 52 12
Hotel Sunwing, Puerto del Carmen: 51 28 55
Hotel La Geria, Playa de los Pocillos, Puerto del Carmen:
51 03 10
Hotel Lanzarote Village, Playa de los Pocillos, Puerto del
Carmen: 51 13 44
Hotel San Antonio, Playa de los Pocillos, Puerto del Carmen:
51 17 57
Hotel Fariones, Calle Roque del Este, Puerto del Carmen:
51 01 75
Amigo el la Perla, Ave. Las Playas, Puerto del Carmen: 82 65 77
Hotel Morromar, Puerto del Carmen: 82 64 04
Hotel Lanzarote Park, Playa Blanca: 51 70 48
Hotel Lanzarote Princess, Playa Blanca: 61 71 08
Hotel Corbeta, Playa Blanca: 51 78 12
Sotavento Club Papagayo, Playa Blanca: 51 71 20

## *Restaurants*

La Jordana, Lanzarote Bay, Costa Teguise: 59 03 28.
Copacabana Garden, Ave. del Mar, Costa Teguise: no telephone
La Chimenea, Las Cucharas, Costa Teguise: no telephone
El Pescador, Pueblo Marinero, Costa Teguise: 59 08 74
Las Cucharas, Costa Teguise: 81 47 00
Chulin, Playa Roca, Costa Teguise: no telephone
La Cañada, Calle General Prime, Puerto del Carmen: 82 64 15
Bahia Tropical, Ave. Las Playas, Puerto del Carmen: no telephone
Playa Mar, Ave. Las Playas, Puerto del Carmen: no telephone
Casta Tino, Calle Nuestra Senora del Carmen, Puerto del
Carmen: no telephone
Tres Copas, Calle Bajamar, Puerto del Carmen: 82 50 06
Timon, Calle Bajamar, Puerto del Carmen: 82 52 21
Castillo de San Jose, Arrecife: 81 30 60

Colon, Calle Matagorda, Puerto del Carmen: 51 25 54
La Paradise Beach, Calle Matagorda, Puerto del Carmen:
51 18 35
Lappland, Calle Los Pocillos, Puerto del Carmen: no telephone
Barcarola, Ave. Las PLayas, Puerto del Carmen: 51 07 75
Pizzeria Capri, Ave. Las Playas, Puerto del Carmen: 51 07 25
Brasil, Calle Los Dragos, Puerto del Carmen: 51 25 65
La Ola, Ave. Las Playas, Puerto del Carmen: 82 60 02
Garden, Calle Columbus, Puerto del Carmen: 82 50 72
Casa Pedro, Playa Blanca: 51 70 22
El Patio, Macher: no telephone

# FUERTEVENTURA
(The island's telephone calling code is 928.)

## Hotels
### Five Stars
Tres Islands, Calle Grandes Playas, Corralejo: 86 60 00
### Four Stars
Los Gorriones, Calle Playa la Barca, Jandia Pajar: 54 70 25
Barlovento, Costa Clama: 64 70 38
Sotavento, Costa Calma: 54 70 41
Riu Maxorata, Calle Mayorca, Jandia: 54 12 30
Riu Calipso, Playa de Jandia, Jandia: 54 12 30
Hotel Bau, SA, Playa de Jandia, Jandia: 54 03 68

## Restaurants
Gran Dragon, Calle de Mayo, Puerto del Rosario: 53 14 51
Frasquita, El Castillo, Caleta de Fuste: no telephone
Molino de Antigua, Antigua: 87 82 20
Club Aguas Verdes, Arrecife:10 83 20
El Patio, Corralejo: no telephone
La Tropicana, Calle General Franco, Corralejo: no telephone

Wolcanostone, Corralejo: no telephone
Sotavento II, Corralejo: 86 61 98
Marisma, Calle La Playa, El Cotillo: no telephone
La Taberna, Costa Calma: no telephone
Restaurante Hoteles Betancuria, Valles de Santa Ines:
no telephone
Victor, Calle Juan Solera, La Playita: 87 09 70
El Poril, Las Playitas: no telephone
Stella Canaris, Jandia: 54 10 51
Charly, Jandia: 54 10 66
Casa Luis, Jandia: 54 12 35
Tabaiba, Jandia: no telephone
Tony Pinte, Jandia: 87 08 43
Montel Del Mar, Jandia: 87 11 88.
Ramon, La Laita: 87 08 49
Laja, Ave. del Mar, Morro Jabla: 54 20 54

# EL HIERRO
(The island's telephone calling code is 922.)

*Hotels*

### Three Stars
Parador Nacional El Hierro, Valverde: 55 01 01
### Two Stars
Boomerang, Calle Doctor Gost, Valverde: 55 02
Hotel Club Puntagrande, Las Puntas, Frontera: 55 90 81
### One Star
Casañas, Calle San Francisco, Valverde: 55 02 54

For information on restaurants, see the "Restaurant" section in the chapter on Hierro.

# LA GOMERA
(The island's telephone calling code is 922.)

*Hotels*

### Four Stars
Hotel Tecina, Playa Santiago: 89 50 50. A new hotel, presently
unrated but likely to have four or five stars.
Parador Conde de la Gomera, San Sebastian: 87 11 00

### One Star
Hotel Canarias, Calle Ruiz de Padrón, San Sebastian: 87 03 55
Hotel Colombina, Calle Ruiz de Padrón, San Sebastian: 87 12 57
Hotel Garajonay, Calle Ruiz de Padrón, San Sebastian: 87 05 50

For information on restaurants, see the "Restaurant" section in the chapter on Gomera.

# GRAN CANARIA
(The island's telephone calling code is 928.)

*Hotels*

### Five Stars
Melia Las Palmas, Calle Gomera, Las Palmas: 26 76 00
Santa Catalina, Parque Doramas, Las Palmas: 24 30 40
Reina Isabel, Calle Alfredo L. Jones, Las Palmas: 26 01 00
Melia Tamarindos, Calle Retama, San Agustin: 76 26 00
Maspalomas Oasis, Plaza del Faro, Maspalomas: 14 14 48
La Canaria, Playa de Puerto Vaca, Arguineguin: 73 60 60

### Four Stars
Sansofe Palace, Paseo las Canteras, Las Palmas: 22 40 66
Bardinos, Calle Eduardo Benot, Las Palmas: 26 61 00
Concorde, Calle Tomas Miller, Las Palmas: 26 27 50
Imperial Playa, Calle Ferreras, Las Palmas: 26 48 54

Rocamar, Calle Lanzarote, Las Palmas: 26 56 00
Iberia, Maritima del Norte, Las Palmas: 38 03 72
Tigaday, Calle Ripoche, Las Palmas: 26 47 20
Don Gregory, Calle Las Cadias, Las Palmas: 76 216 62
Lucana, Plaza del Sol, Playa del Ingles: 76 27 00

Orquidea, Plaza del Tarajalillo, Juan Grande: 76 46 00
Buenaventura, Plaza de Ansire, Playa del Ingles: 76 16 50
Regente, Los Jazmines, San Agustin: 76 09 50
Sunwing, Ave. Gran Canaria, Playa del Ingles: 76 57 12
Estela Polaris, Playa de las Burras, San Agustin: 76 24 80
Gran Canaria Princess, Ave. Gran Canaria, Playa del Ingles:
76 81 32
Gloria Palace, Calle Las Margaritas, San Agustin: 76 83 00
Bahia Mar, La Garita, Telde: 69 16 41
Costa Canaria, Las Retamas, San Agustin: 76 02 00
Sandy Beach, Calle Alferez Provisionales, Playa del Ingles:
76 33 78
Riu Palace, Plaza de Fuerteventura, Playa del Ingles: 76 95 00
Riu Papaya, Ave. de Gran Canaria, Playa del Ingles: 76 50 62
Riu Palmera, Ave. Estados Unidos, Playa del Ingles: 76 64 00
Eugenia Victoria, Ave. de Gran Canaria, Playa del Ingles:
76 25 00
Rey Carlos, Ave. Tirajana, Playa del Ingles: 76 01 16
Las Margaritas, Ave. de Gran Canaria, Playa del Ingles: 76 11 12
Don Miguel, Ave. de Tirajana, Playa del Ingles: 76 15 08
Dunamar, Calle Helsinky, Playa del Ingles: 76 12 00
Apolo, Ave. de Estados Unidos, Playa del Ingles: 76 00 58
Caserio, Ave. de Italia, Playa del Ingles: 76 10 50
Neptuno, Ave. Alferez Provisionales, Playa del Ingles: 76 63 50
Ifa Faro, Faro de Maspalomas, Plaza del Faro, Maspalomas:
14 22 14
Palm Beach, Ave. Oasis, Maspalomas: 14 08 16
Taurito Playa, Playa del Taurito, Mogan: 56 54 00
Paraiso Maspalomas, Ave. Gran Canaria, Playa del Ingles:
76 23 50.

*Restaurants*

Las Cumbres, Ave. Tirajana, Playa del Ingles: 76 09 41,
Compostela, Calle Marcial Franmco, Playa del Ingles: 76 20 92
Rias Bajas, Playa Sol, Playa del Ingles: 76 40 33
Tenderete, Ave. Tirajana, Alohe: 76 14 60
Tropicana, Playa del Ingles: 77 10 34
Anno Domini, San Agustin: 76 18 95
Los Molinos, Ave. Gran Canaria, Playa del Ingles: no telephone
Guantanamo, Mogan: 56 92 63
Cristina, Puerto Rico: 74 62 12
Amayur, Maspalomas: 76 44 14
Duseldorf, Las Palomas: 76 89 81
La Casita, Calle Leon y Castillo, Las Palmas: 23 46 99
Yantar, Ave. Mesa y Lopez, Las Palmas: 26 33 85
Amaiur, Calle Perez Galdos, Las Palmas: 37 07 17
El Padrino, Calle Jesus Nazareno, Las Coloradas: 27 20 94
La Cuadra, Calle General Mas de Gaminde, Las Palmas:
24 33 80
Gourmet, Calle  General Goded, Las Palmas: 23 29 74
El Cerdo que Rie, Calle Las Canteras, Las Palmas: 24 49 54
Marisqueria Muneira, Calle Dr. Grau Bassas: Las Palmas
Casa Galicia, Calle Salvador Cuyas: Las Palmas.

# LA PALMA

(The island's telephone calling code is 922.)

*Hotels*

Parador Nacional de Santa Cruz, Ave. Maritima, Santa Cruz:
41 23 40
Hotel San Miguel, Ave. El Puente, Santa Cruz: 41 12 43
Hotel Canarias, Calle A. Cabera Pinto, Santa Cruz: 41 31 82
Nambroque, Calle Monteluján, El Paso: 48 52 79
La Palma Romántica, Barlovento: 45 08 21
Bahia, Plaza de la Luz, Santa Cruz: 41 18 46

Hotel Eden, Calle Angel, Los Llanos de Aridane: 46 01 04

For La Palma restaurant information, see Being There in the La Palma chapter.

# TENERIFE

(The island's telephone calling code is 922.)

*Hotels*

### Five Stars
Semiramis, Puerto de La Cruz: 38 55 51
San Felipe, Ave. de Colon, Puerto de la Cruz: 38 01 50
Botanico, Puerto de la Cruz: 38 14 00
Sir Anthony, Ave. Maritima, Playa Américas: 79 71 13
Mencey, Calle Doctor José Naveiras, Santa Cruz: 27 67 00
### Four Stars
Abinque, Adeje: 79 42 14
Isla Bonita, Playa de Fañabe, Adeje: 75 00 12
Conquistador, Ave. Litoral, Playa de las Américas: 79 23 99
Guayarmina Princess, Playa de las Américas: 75 15 84
Troya, Ave. Maritima, Playa de las Américas: 79 01 00
Tenerife Sol, Ave. Maritima, Playa de las Américas: 79 10 62
Esmeralda Playa, Adeje: 79 03 78
Colon Guanahani, Adeje: 75 20 46
Gala, Playa de las Americas: 79 45 13
La Siesta, Ave. Maritima, Puerto de las Américas: 79 23 00
Arona Gran Hotel, Los Cristianos, Arona: 75 06 78
Paradise Park, Los Cristianos, Arona: 79 60 11
Los Gigantes, Acantilados de los Gigantes: 86 71 25
Mediterranean Palace, Los Cristianos: 79 40 11
Los Dogos, Calle Granados, Puerto de la Cruz: 38 51 51
Las Aguilas, Las Arenas, Puerto de la Cruz: 38 30 11
Parque San Antonio, Las Arenas, Puerto de la Cruz: 38 48 51
Melia, Puerto de la Cruz: 38 40 11
El Tope, Calzada Martianez, Puerto de la Cruz: 38 40 12

Puerto Palace, Las Arenas, Puerto de la Cruz: 37 24 60
Magec, Calle Perez Zamora, Puerto de la Cruz: 38 55 11
Puerto Playa, Calle Jose Maria del Campo, Puerto de la Cruz:
38 41 51
Miramar, Puerto de la Cruz: 38 48 11
Maritim, Calle Burgados, Los Realejos: 34 20 12
Tigaiga, Plaza Taoro, Puerto de la Cruz: 38 32 51
Internacional, Puerto de la Cruz: 38 51 11
Marquesa, Calle Quintana, Puerto de la Cruz: 38 31 51
Monopol, Calle Quintana, Puerto de la Cruz: 38 46 11
Valle Mar, Ave. Colon, Puerto de la Cruz: 38 47 11
Jardin Tropical, Adeje: 79 41 11
Park Club Europe, Ave. Maritima, Puerto de las Américas:
79 33 98
Santiago, Santiago del Teide: 86 73 75
Atlantis, Ave. Maritima, Puerto Colon: 79 04 08
Vulcano, Playa de las Américas: 79 20 35
Bungaville Playa, Playa de las Américas: 79 02 00
Bitagora, Playa de las Américas: 79 15 40
Torviscas, Playa de las Américas: 79 71 61
Las Dalias, Playa de las Américas: 79 28 09

## *Restaurants*

Magnolia, Puerto de la Cruz: 38 56 14
China II, Ave. Generalisimo, Puerto de la Cruz: 38 19 08
Los Corales, Cuesta la Villa, Santa Ursula: 30 02 49
El Lagar, Cuesta la Villa, Santa Ursula: 30 06 55
El Guanche, Calle Dinamarca, Puerto de la Cruz: 38 58 71
Los Limoneros, Tacoronte: 63 66 37
Cordero Segoviano, La Laguna: 63 61 10
Meson el Drago, Tegueste: 54 30 01
Peruano, Calle del Pozo, Puerto de la Cruz: 38 22 53
Portobello, Calle Los Robles, Puerto de la Cruz: 37 11 42
Mi Vaca y Yo, Calle Cruz Verde, Puerto de la Cruz: 33 52 47
El Coto de Antonio, Calle General Goded, Santa Cruz: 27 21 05

Meson Los Comuneros, Cruce de Boquerón, La Laguna: 63 63 05

Amos, Barrio de Salamanca, Santa Cruz: 28 50 01

Meson los Monjes, Calle La Marina, Santa Cruz: 27 11 83

La Riviera, Rambla General Franco, Santa Cruz: 27 58 12

La Gabarra, Calle Emilio Calzadilla, Santa Cruz: 24 66 02

Los Troncos, Calle General Godet, Santa Cruz: 28 51 52

Portobello II, Calle La Marina, Santa Cruz: 24 79 37

Meson Castellano, Calle Callao de Lima, Santa Cruz: 27 10 74

Casa Ramallo, La Esperanza: 26 32 02

Mi Casita, Arafo: 50 09 88

La Hoya del Camello, La Laguna: 26 20 54

Don Antonio, San Andrés: 54 96 73

Restaurante Hotel Mencey, Rambla General Franco, Santa Cruz: 27 67 00

Cafeteria Olympo, Plaza de la Candelaria, Santa Cruz: 24 25 77

Mama Rosá, Centro Comercial Colon, Playa de las Américas: 79 48 19

Folias, Pueblo Canario, Pláya de las Américas: 79 22 69

Parque de las Americas, Playa de las Américas: 79 76 11

Don Pancho, Playa de las Américas: 86 83 30

Las Rejas, Arona: 72 08 94

La Langostera, Granadilla: 17 63 19

Banana Garden, Playa de las Américas: 79 03 65

Casa Vasca, Playa de las Américas: 79 32 03

Casa del Mar, Arona: 79 32 75

La Fragua, Arona: 78 57 38

El Patio, Hotel Jardin Tropical, Adeje: 79 41 11

THE ROQUES DE GARCIA ARE ONE OF THE MOST
POPULAR TOURIST DESTINATIONS ON MT. TEIDE.
THE RUGGED ROCKS ARE PROBABLY THE MOST
PHOTOGRAPHED SPOT IN THE CANARIES.

CARLOS LOZANO PEREZ, THE WINEMAKER IN THE
TASTING ROOM AT BODEGAS TENEGUIA ON LA PALMA.

LOOKING DOWN ON THE COLONIAL CITY OF LA
OROTAVA, NEAR THE CAPITAL OF SANTA CRUZ ON
TENERIFE.

ONE OF THE MANY BEAUTIFUL WHITE SAND BEACHES
OF GRAN CANARIA.

CAVES ON THE NORTH COAST OF GRAN CANARIA
WHERE THE GUANCHES BURIED THEIR DEAD.

A STEEP CANYON WITH TERRACED
VINEYARDS ON THE ISLAND OF GOMERA.

THE ATLANTIC
CRASHES AGAINST
THE ROCKY SHORE
ON THE ISLAND
OF HIERRO.

THE SPECTACULARLY BEAUTIFUL CALDERA DE
TABURIENTE ON LA PALMA.

A GOLDEN DESSERT WINE
FROM THE ISLAND OF LA PALMA

WINDSURFING IS EXCELLENT IN THE CANARY ISLANDS.

**LAS VERESITAS BEACH NORTH OF SANTA CRUZ
ON TENERIFE.**

A TYPICAL CANARIAN BALCONY IN THE COLONIAL
TOWN OF LA OROTAVA ON THE ISLAND OF TENERIFE.

A DRAGON TREE WITH MT. TEIDE IN THE BACK-
GROUND IN THE WINEGROWING CENTER OF ICOD ON
TENERIFE.

TRADITIONAL
COSTUMES ARE
OFTEN WORN
DURING THE
CARNAVAL
CELEBRATIONS
IN THE CANARIES.